# God Talk

By Sally Love, M. A.

# DEDICATION

**This book is dedicated to you, my reader, with my love and hope that it will strengthen your connection to our Heavenly Father God.**

# INTRODUCTION

This book includes 310 numbered prayers; one for nearly every day of the year, except Sundays. The entries are numbered rather than dated, because it is more important that you read and keep reading than that you stay with a calendar. It is written as a tool to connect you to God. Because a prayer that isn't spoken is just a thought, this book will be most effective for you if it is read aloud. Reading aloud will best connect your heart to God. Feel free to stop and add to each prayer as you come to the end of it. Share your deepest thoughts and hurts with the ONE who will be delighted to hear from you! There is some room on most pages to add your own thoughts. Each prayer ends with asking God, "What do you want me to know, Father? Please listen at that point?

**Day 1**

Father God,

I ask You to speak into my life what I need to achieve complete transformation of character and perfection of my soul? Please clean up my attitude, realign my purpose and keep me moving to the goal of fulfilling Your high calling in my life?

Let me be a better servant? Show me how to sacrifice myself on the altar of Your work? Teach me what things I need to set aside and what I need to lose forever. Show me the plan You have for me? Lead me in the path of righteousness? Let me be after Your own heart—a worker that need not be ashamed, rightly dividing the word of truth. Teach me Your ways and put Your words in my heart? Let me speak as apples of gold and pitchers of silver? Create in me a clean heart and renew in me a clean and right spirit?

Father, You are so awesome! Thank You for letting me come to You with these requests! Thank You for doing what I need in every situation! I ask You in Jesus' name to help me as I grow to know You better. What do You want me to know today, Father?

**Day 2**

Father God,

I notice that I am so easily distracted. Will You please help me turn off the distractions and focus on You? Help me see immediately which activities are not bringing life to me? And help me to separate from them?

Please, help me to be the servant You purchased with the blood of Jesus, Your son? Help me deny myself and take up my cross.

I need You so much. I want to be with You so much. I want to be a worker, fully-functional and completely yielded. There are so many hurt and wounded people in this world. Please show me what I can do to share Your love and healing with them? Bring me to conformity. Put me in a narrow strait so I can't stray. Put the necessary money into my hands so I can complete the job You have for me?

Father, please conform me to Your image? Place Your hand on my heart and squeeze out the evil and the unlovely? Don't let me fail You? Don't let me fall short of all You have called me to do? Put a guard on my tongue? Fill my heart with scripture and spill it out instead of the foulness of my past? Remove from me every unclean thing, Lord? Set me free from besetting sins and blind me to temptation? In Jesus' name, I ask these things. What do You want me to know today, Father?

**Day 3**

Father God,

Great is Your faithfulness! Great is Your mercy! You are the essence of my life.

Thank You for the love and grace You have shown me all these years. Thank You for the patience and mercy You have given to me. You are so indescribably great in every category! You are the creator of creativity, the designer of life itself, the eternal essence and the divine contributor of all our needs. Thank You! Thank You! No one can come near Your goodness!

Beyond our paltry existence, surpassing our human limitations, extending far beyond our dreams, You sit supreme. Thank You! Please help me to help others? I am so frustrated with the pace of hurry up and wait. There are so many people who need healing and need to be taught. Please help the one I love? She is so wounded, played out, worn out and physically exhausted. But You know all that. Please do all that You know to be best for her?

I need You. I want You. Please heed and answer my prayer? I ask in Jesus' name? What do You want me to know today, Father?

**Day 4**

Father God,

Thank You for letting me know what is important to know. Thank You for helping me grow and learn. You are so wonderful. You are overwhelming me with Your love more every day. You enrich me and You bless me all the time. Without You, I am nothing. Yours is an eternal, wholesome, healthy, complete love. Thank You for loving me so much! I have so much on my mind today, please heed my requests?

I plead with You, Father, in Jesus' name, that You will help the discouraged and weary Christians in this world. Please send them the money they need, the food they need, the exact clothing they need, and the spiritual encouragement they need. Please open the eyes of the saints on earth? Let all of us see clearly and learn quickly.

Please show me if there is anything I must do in my marriage? What do You want me to do? Show me what to do everyday in every category, please? Help me accomplish all that You need me to do? Please help me memorize the verses You gave me? Please, I know I don't deserve healing, but please make me completely whole and well? Forgive me? I am tired and so weary. I have much to learn and much to release. Please help me release all things to Your care?

I ask these things in Jesus' name. What do You want me to know today, Father?

**Day 5**

Dearest Father,

Thank You for showing me the keys to the kingdom. Help me to know what You want me to do with them? Help me to remember them? I need You. I need Your help. I need Your wisdom. You are the reason I love and the reason I am able to understand everything. Thank You for revealing truth to me.

No one knows me like You do, Father. Please fix the things that are wrong and the things that need adjusted in me? Please help me to recognize my sins and to confess them to You daily? I am a fool if I presume that I have no sins, I can see the fruit in my life. Please help me find the roots of bitterness, the lies of the enemy and the grudges I bear? Show me my self-righteousness? I am so human! Please forgive me and help me? I need You! I need Your wisdom and Your correction! I can't see myself as others do and I can't be all I need to be if I keep the junk in me. Please help me see the sin and hear when others try to help me? Help me to surrender this stubborn will to Your purpose and Your plan for my life? I ask in Jesus' name that You help me every way that You can. What do You want me to know today, Father?

**Day 6**

Father of all creation,

I adore You! Thank You for the marvelous day You have given me! You are God of all and all I need. Your will is my choice and my desire. I will seek You this and every day. I choose You. I trust Your wisdom and plan. I yield to Your purpose for me, whatever that may be. You are beyond description! God, You rule!

Speak clearly that I may hear You? Remove from me every block that would hinder my obedience. Lead me in the only path that will bring me to full function as an extension of Your arm?

There is nothing that I need that You don't know about. But there are people who do need Your help. For that reason, in Jesus' name, I ask that You bless and increase them. Please teach them, train them and bring them to great spiritual growth? Set them free from their besetting sins, their iniquities, their fears and every other hindrance to their growth. Work within them to install a love for Your word and Your work? Provide for their physical, spiritual and emotional needs. Strengthen them as they continue to call on You and grow. Grant them wisdom and courage. I ask all this in Jesus' name. What do You want me to know today, Father?

**Day 7**

Father God,

I need You! I want You! You are my source of strength. You are my courage, my knowledge, my wisdom and my future. More than anything else, I want to serve You full-time. I want to be an open conduit of Your love. I need to know and do Your will every day for the rest of my life.

Because You are so wonderful, You are fulfilling. You are enriching. It is Your wisdom that keeps me going and keeps me growing. Please, don't ever turn off the pipeline? Please, don't let me separate myself from You? I need Your fullness.

In Jesus' name, I ask You to teach and train all the ones I love and even more so—the ones You love! Please help every one on the planet to find You? Continue to lead the lost to repentance? Please make it as easy as possible for Christians in restricted countries to learn from You? Send them Your word via the voices of strangers and even their enemies? Speak to them through print media, television, satellite, radio, computer, visions, and directly by angels and the Holy Spirit. I ask You to send every available angel, fully-armored, supplied and with war tools to fight the enemy's hosts and win every battle. What do You want me to know today, Father?

**Day 8**

Father God,

You are so cool! You are unbelievably beyond measurability! I worship You! I need You. Your plan and purpose are so exact and so perfect. Thank You for Your love and grace and mercy. Thank You for providing for me daily. Thank You for my children. Thank You for this home that has kept me safe and warm. You are my solution, my director and my goal. All that at I am, I owe to You. All that I see, I owe to You because I'll never have anything without You. I love You. You never fail me. You never let me down. You never hurt me. You don't abuse me or use me.

No one cares for me like You do. You make me feel desired, cherished and valuable. NO one could replace You in my heart and life.
Please don't take Your love from me? Don't separate me from You? Don't even let me walk away? I need You! I love You.

Thank You for knowing my needs and meeting them so well and so completely. Thank You for the treats You have given me! I love the fact that You allow me to get my sugar fixes when I need them. You are so cool! What do You want me to know today, Father?

**Day 9**

Father God,

I trust You!

Above all things in my life, I trust and ask that You will direct all that I do. You alone are able. God, You are the coolest, most loving, most wonderful, and the only perfect being that ever was seen. I love You! To know You is to love You and adore You! Your will is a pleasure to do!

Because of Your perfect plan for a perfect creation, I am a fully functioning part of Your purpose, whether or not I comprehend the full scope of my life. For that fact—me being a part of Your plan—I thank You, love You and appreciate You so much! You are so wonderful to me! When I see the mess I make of myself, I appreciate the fact that eternity will be spent with You. I love the fact that You have it all worked out and that all will be working according to plan. I love the fact that You will let me make mistakes and then use them to teach me such eternal truths! Thank You for leading me and keeping me safe and on track! You are incredible beyond measure. Before the first idea in the universe, You existed! What a comfort to know that You are well and You will never end.

Father, I love You. What do You want me to know today, Father?

**Day 10**

Father,

You are so cool!  You let me explore so many wonderful ideas.  Thank
You for teaching me and bringing me to the point where I can help others.  You
are awesome!  Your ways are so much higher than mine!  You are so able and
so ready to let us learn.  Thank You for letting humans have input into other
humans!

Oh God, Your goodness is beyond measure and beyond what we deserve
by a million miles.  You are the best; You are better than all the rest.  Your life
has given us blessing after blessing.  Human vocabulary cannot begin to express
the magnitude of Your generosity and goodness to us.  You are the king of kings
and Lord of lords, but yet You care about me!  You are incredible!  I love You
immensely, totally and fervently.  You are my one and only reason for living
and You are my peace and my joy.  I admire You, I need You and I want Your
presence.  In all ways, at all times, I am indebted to You and Your mercy and
grace.  You rule!  What do You want me to know today, Father?

**Day 11**

Father God,

All of my days I will praise You. Always, in every endeavor I will give You the credit. You are the only God, the always God, the God of Gods and King of Kings! I need You! I want You! You alone are worthy of my undivided devotion.

I repent of wasting time, using Your time unwisely and devoting myself to self-entertainment. Help me make my life changes, please? In Jesus' name, please help me change my life and devote myself to You full-time? Please set me free from hindrances to Your love? Set me free from things that would keep me from serving You full-time. Please, help me renounce my sins forever?

No one understands me. No one recognizes what You are doing in me. No one knows what You mean to me. Please, in Jesus' name, give me an outlet in which to teach and express Your love? Help me help others? There are so many people who would be better if they could be helped to maturity and growth. Please let me help other people who know less about You than I do?

I know You know what is best for me. Please show me what to do next? Please guide me? I ask all this in Jesus' name. What do You want me to know today, Father?

**Day 12**

Father God,

  You are so incredible, so far beyond description and so full of power and grace. God, You are beautiful beyond description, too marvelous for words. Beyond all human comprehension, more than I've ever seen or heard, God, I love You. I adore You. You are the God of all creation, the maker of all substance. You are the origin and the originator of all things. Nothing, absolutely nothing, altogether nothing is too difficult for You. Your mercies are new every morning.

  Your kindness leads me to repentance when Your judgment could destroy or terminate me. My future is in Your hands. Be merciful to me, a sinner. I need Your grace. I need Your presence. I covet Your love. Hold me in Your heart and keep me in Your arms? Protect me as only You can? You are so beautiful to me! You are so wonderful to me! You are absolutely, positively, all-encompassing, all-enclosing, omniscient, omnipresent and loving. Your capacity frustrates my descriptive abilities. I love You, God. What do You want me to know today, Father?

**Day 13**

Father God,

Thank You for today. Thank You for being so incredibly awesome! Thank You for Your kindness that leads me to repentance. Thank You that Your mercy lets me live during the bad years and still today. Thank You for the clues You give me to Your greatness.

You are always kind, good, loving, helpful, generous, merciful and full of power. You are in me in fullness, strength and without weakness. You are in me to strengthen me, empower me, work through me and guide me. You rule with gentleness and love! You are the modeler and remodeler of our universe! You have structured my life and continue to shape it daily. You keep me safe and You keep me feeling safe! All the positive words from all the languages used at once couldn't begin to describe Your goodness. Your majesty overflows. Your purpose is perfect. You plan is flawless. Mighty, mighty God! You are the one we all adore.

Thank You for letting me laugh, letting me talk, and letting me lean on You, although I don't deserve it. The more I know You the more I need You. Holy, holy, holy God, I surrender to Your plans, purpose and structure. What do You want me to know today, Father?

**Day 14**

Father God,

You are so cool! You gave us so many wonderful colors! Your love is like a composite of pleasant visions and a restful stream. Your love is a precious and never-ending delight. No one will ever know the full depth of Your being. No one can begin to comprehend the full extent of Your existence.

Thank You for noticing me and loving me. Thank You for mentoring me. You have taught me so many things. I love You for that!

Your goal is my destiny. Your plan is my purpose. Never in my own mind could I begin to plan for Your mission to be accomplished. Please, help me see Your daily, step-by-step plan for my life? I need to know so much. Help me not to presume to know what is most important? Help me to know and do Your will, Father? Every plan I make is subject to Your approval. Help me to not make plans? Help me to seek You for Your plan for my life? Your plans are flawless, complete and perfect for every situation. No one can devise an original plan; it's all been done. Help me not to be deceived by thinking that what I have is original? Help me do only what You would have done? I ask in Jesus' name. What do You want me to know today, Father?

**Day 15**

Father God,

I need You! You are always reliable. You will never fail me or disappoint me. Thank You for not being like humans! Thank You for never using or abusing me! You are incredible—You know what I am and still love me. I don't understand Your plan and purpose but I know it is the wisest for me. I want You! I don't know why I chose such a hard life for myself. I don't know why anyone would! Of all the things in my life, I am most grateful that You help me everyday. I whip myself daily with my bad judgment, but I am confident that every word of scripture is true. And because of that, I know You are sanctifying me.

Holy Lord God, worthy and blessed One, You rule in majesty and glory. Your honor supersedes even our concept of honor. Your love is magnified far beyond our puny concept of love. Now and forever You are the Commander of the Army, the Captain of the Hosts, the Father of all. What can I begin to do that will repay You for all that You do for me? Teach me, Father, teach me. Organize me. Rebuke me. Correct me. Deliver me from selfishness and ambition. Establish Your work and show me my role in it. In Jesus' name I ask. What do You want me to know today, Father?

**Day 16**

Father God,

You are so good. You are pure, holy and glorious! You have no faults, no failures and no mistakes!

I am so sorry. I have let the events of this life take me from the work You want me to do. Please forgive me for wasting time speaking of things I can't change? Please help me focus on my study and my purpose? I don't want to look back at my life and say, "I meant to do a lot of things for You." I used to beg You to use me, but I never applied myself to prepare myself to be used. I have become a wasted life. Thirty years of spirit-filled pity party. I am no better than the ones I judge. I want to live as a useful vessel—not a waste of good dust. Please, help me simplify my life and put my life in order? My life needs structure and deliberate planning. Please help me make a plan and work the plan? Help me get the house in order and keep it in order? I don't want anyone to walk in and be uncomfortable in my home ever.

I need You! I want You! I need to establish my days so that Your will is accomplished in my life. Thank You for tolerating me. Thank You for giving me grace and mercy. No being can compare to Your infinite goodness! I love You and ask Your help and mercy in Jesus' name. What do You want me to know today, Father?

**Day 17**

Father God,

Please direct us? You are so awesome, kind, loving and creative. You alone know the path You have planned for us. You know what is best for us better than we can imagine. Your wisdom exceeds our needs and imagination. Your purpose extends far more deeply and broadly than we can imagine. You are God!

We plan, set goals, and endeavor in vain unless You complete Your work through us. No one knows what You have planned for our eternity. Let us surrender fully to all that You have for us? Let us give all that we have to be all that You need. No one can begin to unravel the threads of our own lives without You. I am so tired of being a pile of knotted string, useless and ugly. Please unravel me and rewind me? Use me for Your glory, please? We all need You. We all want things and to be a pleasure for You. We all want to give back to You. Please help us all to give back? I ask in Jesus' name. What do You want me to know today, Father?

**Day 18**

Father God,

Awesome incredible God! You are so far beyond description! You supersede language!

Creative, generous, loving, wise, good Father, You are the best. You always know what is best for us. You save us, teach us, bless us and love us despite what we are! You have all power and all creation in Your hand and yet You never close the fist and eliminate us worthless sinners. You can do as You will and yet You do not destroy us and You seem to do nothing but what brings us growth and life. I love You so much! I am so dependent on Your mercy and grace. The day in and day out events of my life show me my helplessness and dependence on You. Please don't fail me? No one knows the extent of my sins and all assess the maximum penalty. Please intervene to provide for me? I desire above all to bring glory and honor to You. I ask in Jesus' name. Thank You for all that You have done for me. Thank You that I'm not abused. Thank You for letting me know You as my Lord and Master. I love You and I appreciate You so much! Nobody knows me like You know me. Nobody loves me like You love me. You are so cool! What do You want me to know today, Father?

**Day 19**

Father God,

Thank You for giving me ideas. I love how You bless me with so many neat ideas! You are the most creative of us all—thank You for sharing some of that creativity with us. You are so wise. I trust You to make my decisions, direct my path, and stop me from making major mistakes. You are my hope and my future. You rule!

I find myself in the desert between Sinai and Egypt. Where do I turn next? What do I do next? What is Your plan for me? Should I begin again where You took me out? Please help all Christians in my situation? Help them to know exactly what You want them to do? My desire is to work for You. Help me work for You? Let me work full-time for You? I am so untrained. I want to train but I am not trained. Help me to be wise in my plans and ambitions? Speak to me, Father, I need to hear from You. I need to be directed by You. I can't lead myself. Help me! In Jesus' name, I ask. What do You want me to know today, Father?

**Day 20**

Father God,

Thank You for being so much more than I ever expected! You are wonderful, delightful, desirable, excellent and energetic. I admire You, appreciate You, recognize You and need You. You are better than excellence and greater than the greatest. All of the days of my life will be filled with thoughts of You. You are the love in my heart and the hope I feel. I have no promises I can trust but Yours. I have no hope beyond eternity. You are my goal, my purpose and my future. You will always be the only one I can rely on fully.

Father, You love me when I don't deserve life. You tolerate me when no one should. I need Your help. I need discretion. I need to have both discretion and tact. Please give them to me? I am a bad voice to some people. I don't want to be offensive to anyone for any reason. Please help me not to speak out of turn? I want to speak only when it is apples of gold and pitchers of silver. Enable me to be Your voice of comfort and encouragement? Enable me to be an exhorter of the brethren? Let me be Your conduit of peace?

Your will is perfect. Your plans are without flaws. Your purpose will be fulfilled. Holy, holy, holy, God, I love You. What do You want me to know today, Father?

**Day 21**

Father God,

Thank You for loving me. Thank You for taking me out of my funk today. I appreciate You all day every day. I love You, Lord God. I honor You. I recognize Your power and Your powers. Blessed be Your glorious name forever!

Forgive me for sinning with my mouth today. I sinned and I want to stop it. Forgive me for judging my mother? Forgive me for judging my father? Forgive me for believing my father abandoned me? I know now that You have never abandoned me. No one is capable of healing me but You, God. Please heal me and create in me a clean heart? Restore unto me the joy of Your salvation. Renew a right spirit within me? Help me die to myself? Help me to completely surrender my life to You? Please set Your plan in motion in my life? Please get Your purpose fulfilled in me? Show me Your way, God. Teach me Your will. Lead me in paths of righteousness for Your name's sake.

For You and You alone I am eager. I need Your presence. I need Your love. Be with me. Come to me. Get through to me. I ask all this in Jesus' name. What do You want me to know today, Father?

**Day 22**

Father God,

Thank You for a good day—for letting me actually work for hours! Thank You for being there and being my strength. You are so awesome!! You rule!! You are on time, ready, fully prepared and thinking ahead! You're great!

Thank You for blessing that boy today. Thank You for knowing that he wanted a soda and for letting me give it to him. It was an impulse I thought was mine; to see that You were answering his desire through me was awesome. Awesome God! All knowing ruler! All provident lover of mankind, You are too cool!

I am so gratefully tired after the work today. Thank You for the many blessings that came. Thank You for the blessing of different food today. You are too cool. You are God. You are the one and only God. I love You.

I ask You to please keep my children safe for their trip. Please let me sleep well and awake with no soreness from the work? Please do these things? I ask in Jesus' name. What do You want me to know today, Father?

**Day 23**

Father God,

Your love is better than anything I could wish for.  I need You    I want You.  You are so good to me.

Help me get free of all my entanglements?  Free from my besetting sins and iniquities?  Please?  In all my ways, all of my days, I will continue to strive to reach You.

We all need You!  And we all want Your presence more than life itself. Let me know and feel You more than I ever have before.  Let me learn without obstacles.  Help me free myself from my addictions?

Today I ask in Jesus' name that You send comfort to every child of Yours that is in prison for the cause of Christ.  I ask You to supernaturally send food to every hungry Christian—wherever they may be in the world.  Send encouragement to all the hurting Christians, please?  Please send truth to the Muslims and Islamic peoples?  Please clarify Your truth in my life, also?

Send out Your angels tonight to do warfare with the enemy.  Send them fully armed, prepared, munitioned and in ranks.  Tear down strongholds, defeat lies, overcome obstacles to truth.  Win for our side, God.  Now, tonight, win for us.  I ask these things in Jesus' name. What do You want me to know today, Father?

**Day 24**

Father God,

I need to know You! I need to love You! I want You. I know that You love me and want what is best for me. Today, everyday and forever You will be incomparable! Your organizational skill is massive! Your planning is incredible. Your love is too wonderful. No one ever did what You do everyday better than anyone could ever conceive of doing. You rock!

Thank You for today and all that You do for me everyday. Thank You for the great catfish lunch. Thank You for good coffee. You are so cool! YOU rule! Now is the day appointed by You for all of us to serve and give. Thank You for allowing us to do that! You are so generous—we appreciate You!

No one anywhere has even thought of thinking about the work You do everyday. Being Your child is the easiest thing I do. I fail You everyday but I know You forgive me and have patience for me. Thank You!

Cleanse me? Set me free? Remove from me the desire to sin? On the authority of Jesus' name I ask You to reveal and remove every stronghold in me. Loose me from every hindering thing so I can be free to fully serve You, please? What do You want me to know today, Father?

**Day 25**

Almighty Father,

God of heaven and earth, leader of all, You are the source of all joy and peace. You rule triumphantly over all kingdoms. Yours is the power and the glory forever and ever. I trust You to do all that needs doing in the earth and in my life. And I ask You to show me all that I need to know to have my character formed completely. Let me know You and be all that You need me to be. Please help me? Please fix the wounds in my heart? Will You please work on me until I am all that You need me to be? Your will is my purpose and goal. I need to do what You want me to do. Help me get there? Help me be what You want me to be? No one ever succeeded at Your will without Your help. Help me! Show me why I feel I need to be in control and why I have to take care of everything.

What is my block? Why can't I remember what it is? Thank You for letting me remember the areas where I need healing.

You are so cool! I love You! AWESOME God! Please do these things for me? I ask in Jesus' name? What do You want me to know today, Father?

**Day 26**

Father God,

Thank You for a great weekend and good movies. I love You! It's nice to know You let me have things that I really enjoy. I'm sorry if I let them get in Your way. Please forgive me?

You are awesome. You originate, create and reform us all. You are the source of all sources. You create the original parts of all things. You care for all of us. You care for the unlovely. You care for the ones with the most pain.

In Jesus' name, I ask You to help me learn to help hurting people. Teach me what I need to know to not hurt anyone any further.

When I am down, You lift me up. You are my hope when I have none. No one knows where the real hurt is. Please heal all the hurting ones? Help the ones on the outside of Your church. Help the ones who learn how to do it right, then move, and suddenly it's all wrong. Help all the new ones, the kids who feel they stand out in the crowd. Help all children, please?

Father, the world is full of hurting people, please let Jesus come soon? We need Jesus to come back. Please let Him come?

I want to be with You. I need You. I love You. Hold me? What do You want me to know today, Father?

**Day 27**

Father God,

I'm so tired! Thank You for never getting too tired to listen.

I'm curious about me. What good does it do me to have a performer's desire to show off? What is that all about? I don't have an audience and don't want one now. I'd rather speak Your word and read Your word and teach than make them laugh. Sometimes I can't help myself, I just come out funny. What is that about? Nobody wants to hear from an old fat lady and I have nothing to say. Oh well, it's all in Your hands anyway. At this point I'd be happy if I could help people laugh a little.

I can remember being a teenager and wanting to be funny. It was a way to get attention. I'm sorry if I hogged the rooms a bit. I'm sorry if I need too much attention. Please fix that in me?

I look at all the things that You have done for me and I'm so impressed. You created the entire set of universes and still You speak to me! Wow! Thanks for the laughs from the TV tonight. I'm so glad You gave us a sense of humor. Someday, I'll bet I'll get to hear jokes in Heaven. Thank You and goodnight! What do You want me to know today, Father?

**Day 28**

Father God,

Tonight will You send forth all Your warring angels to do battle for our side? Take back lives, homes, territories and children for us? Speak forth truth to all the deceived ones. I ask You to arrange victory in lands where Your name is not exalted. I ask You to organize troops of Christian warriors that will march forward in prayer and praise to claim the victory for our side. I know that we will win the war, but I ask You to let us win battles from now on. Let us take back homes, schools, hospitals, nations and people groups. So many of our side have been wounded by the enemy already and are deceived. Help them find truth? Help all the wounded ones to find You? Please step forth in power and reveal Yourself to the world. Let us all feel Your love and forgiveness? Let us all feel Your mercy and grace? Let no one doubt that You exist and that You are working for our good and for our future.

You are so awesome and so good! I pray that everyone may experience Your goodness and faithfulness to us. Let us all know how good it is to be with You. I ask in Jesus' name. What do You want me to know today, Father?

**Day 29**

Father God,

You are always right, brave, compassionate, truthful, kind and perfect. It is foolishness in us to attempt to be any of these things. You are so capable.

Will You please help me grow in self-control? I need to eat less, focus more, watch less TV and walk more. Please help me—I ask in Jesus' name. And Father, please protect my son? Keep him safe from himself and others? Watch over him to protect his spirit and his heart? Please speak to him to give him direction and a goal? He needs You so much. Please help him? Lead him in paths of righteousness. I pray now for both of my children. I bless them in Jesus' name in the areas of health, wisdom, peace, prosperity and love for others.

Thank You for letting me get my work done. Please let tomorrow be a good day? And Father, help me finish the work You have given me. I want to work on it and finish it so You will be glorified. Continue to supply all my needs. I ask in Jesus' name for all these requests. And please, use me to reach lost and hurting people? What do You want me to know today, Father?

**Day 30**

Father God,

Thank You for all that You do. I am constantly amazed by what happens when I honor You and ask You to "do what is best for this person today". I love to watch You work!

! I love it that every time I pray, asking You to choose what is best for the person, something different—but wonderful and right—happens! I know it doesn't happen because I ask; it happens because You want to bless them and You always know what is best for them! I would have chosen healing for the person, but You knew peace was more important. Thank You for always being wiser than we are!

I'm just beginning to be amazed at the different results from the same prayer! I wonder at Your ability in amazement and befuddlement because You go right to the heart of the matter every time! Cool, awesome, perfect, righteous, faithful God! You are so far beyond life and what we think we need or should have. You do so much for our eternal good that has nothing to do with right now! Thank You for not answering our hearts and for being the father You are—the one who does what is best regardless of what we think! What do You want me to know today, Father?

**Day 31**

Father God,

Thank You for always choosing what is best for us! I would have chosen a
new car the day I bought the car I drove today. But then when I lost my job it
would have been lost also. Instead I have a car that runs well and is still going,
minus reverse, but hey, it's paid for! You know me and my situation better than
I know myself. I have wanted so many things so many times that would not
have been good for me at all. You know what will be best in the long haul.
Thank You for taking care of me the best way.

I'm not a good shopper at all. It is just now getting into my head that as
smart as I think I am—obviously smarter than reality—I am not a good shopper!
I go and grab the first thing I see and then when I get it home, I'm disappointed!
You are so good to provide for me anyway! Why is it that with all my
experience I mess up when it comes to me? I choose poorly and always have
made decisions about myself that were not in my own best interest. I have never
availed myself of the covering You provided for me, have I? I could have
listened to my husband and been so much better off in life. At least in some
issues I'd have been better. Why is it that we fight Your choices and want to
cling to the ones we make? Is it an issue of rebellion or are we just assuming
that we—feeble minded and puny as we are—actually think that we know better
than You? Forgive me, Father, for my presumption of superiority? Please help
me to recognize when I am exerting my will over Your blessing? I ask in Jesus'
name that You do these things. What do You want me to know today, Father?

**Day 32**

Father God,

Thank You for all that You do for me. You are awesome in every category! Your plan is extremely far beyond comprehension! Your ability is superlative beyond superlative. Incredible and baffling, inspirational and intriguing, Your level of operation exceeds my capacity to describe it!

I know that I can trust You to do all that I need. I know that Your supply is unlimited, unrestricted and self-renewing. Whoa! You are so AWESOME! You rule! You can do all that has ever been done and yet You talk to me! I don't deserve Your love! I don't deserve even Your attention. If I could bless You I would! No one can give back anything for all the love You bless us with. The scales are irreversibly tipped to Your side, which makes You even more awesome! I need more words to describe You! English just doesn't do it!

I love to be with You. I love to write to You and talk to You. I can count on You to never hurt me.

Thank You for reminding us of Your love and Your power.

Please come soon—I miss You! What do You want me to know today, Father?

**Day 33**

Father God,

You are immeasurably bountiful! You enrich us! You bless us. You strengthen us. Your strength is excessively wonderful. No one can match Your power or purpose. You rule with wisdom and majesty. When all the money and jewels and precious metals on Earth are gathered and counted, they will still be worthless and totally valueless compared to You. There is nothing on Earth that even compares to Your glory.

Awesome! Incredible! Beneficent God! Benevolent, loving, kind and generous God! You are the source of my sources. You encourage us, provide and cover us and You prepare and serve us.

You are the source for my needs. You fill me, heal me, wash me, and cleanse me. You make me whole!

You are my forever God, the destiny I long for. You are the goal of my ambition and the reward of all my effort. Your will and purpose and plan are perfect! In You there is no flaw, fault, failure or lack. You are complete and beautiful in every way. Describing and praising You, God, is my impossible task. I love You. I need You. I want You. Thank You for the love You swathe us with daily. Thank You for letting Your son die for me. What do You want me to know today, Father?

**Day 34**

Father God,

You are strong and capable. You are incredible and wise. God, Your power is beyond our comprehension. You rule!

Every time I think of You I am comforted. You are a safe place in every storm. You are a haven for the storms of my life. Thank You for always being there for me and for holding me. Thank You for being my refuge in life and my comforter. Yes, even though I must walk through the valley of the shadow of death, You will go with me. Your love encompasses me and keeps me warm. You are my hope and shelter. Thank You for preparing me. Thank You for warning me.

Father, I ask You in Jesus' name for mercy for our nation. In every storm, please spare as many lives as You can? Help as many hurting people as You can? Father, please tell us as much as You can as far ahead as You can? Let us know what You can? Prepare people for the loss of their loved ones? Please don't take my loved ones? I know that no one goes home until it is their time, please help us remember that Heaven is a better place? Your power is impressive and greater than the enemy. You hold all power, all strength! You control all! You orchestrate our lives. Let Your will be done and Your purpose fulfilled! What do You want me to know today, Father?

**Day 35**

Father God,

You are so strong and wise! You direct me and help me every day. Your plan is on a scale that is beyond our comprehension. Thank You for letting us see glimpses of Your greatness. When I look up and see the complexity of Your work, I marvel at the intricacies that are necessary. You connect all of us with Your love and You do it so we can grow and become more like You. The more I know about You, the more I want to know You. The deeper I relate to You, the deeper I want to be in You.

Thank You for Your patience! You are so full of mercy and grace toward me. Thank You for extending me one more day, one more chance, and one more opportunity than I deserve! I am so frequently wrong. I am so often in the wrong place at the wrong time. Please forgive me for not doing what You need me to do? Help me be what You need me to be?

No one knows me like You do. No one loves me like You do. Just the fact that You love me blesses me so much! Thank You for letting me know You and talk to You. I need You! Forgive me for my failures? Fix my strongholds, please? I ask all this in Jesus' name. What do You want me to know today, Father?

**Day 36**

Father God,

You are the one and only perfect God. You rule better than the best. Your love is deeper, wider, more expansive and more complete than anything I could even begin to describe.

All of my dreams are tied up in You. All of my hopes are wound up in Your plans for my life. You direct me, empower me and enable me. You strengthen me day in and day out. I can count on You, God, when all others fail me. You never hurt me or grow tired of me. You are my hope and my salvation.

Thank You, God! Thank You for all that You do for me. I appreciate and honor You. No one meets my needs like You do. No one cares for me and loves me like You do. No one knows my future but You, God. No one can see my future and know that there is hope in it but You.

I see Your power and purpose and I'm ashamed that I fail You so often. Please forgive me? Let me be with You? Let me walk with You always? I love You. What do You want me to know today, Father?

**Day 37**

Father God,

Show me how I can help the church help the hurting? No one knows how much the wounded ones are hurting but You, God. No one knows how to best help them but You. Please help them? Turn their sorrow into joy, Father. Let them know and experience Your power in every situation, Lord God. Be the strength they need, please? You alone know what has really happened and how to do what will make them grow. Help everyone to grow and mature in these painful situations?

You are my all-powerful, all-mighty, wise and wonderful God. You rule!

Thank You for the love and the mercy You show to me everyday. Thank You for the blessing tonight. You are awesome and so good.

Please give me more money so I can give it to places that need it. I know it is selfish to want to be the giver. I know You like to give direct. Please, You choose. Will You bless the adults and the children directly or will You let me? I love to give, too.

Father, please supply all that is needed to reach the children of our world? I ask all of the things in Jesus' name. What do You want me to know today, Father?

**Day 38**

Father God,

I am so glad that You are in charge! You are so glorious! Let Your name be magnified. You rule with honor and dignity. Be exalted, O God, above the heavens. Be exalted far above all things! You are worthy and holy and powerful! Be exalted, O God, in all the Earth!

Blessed is the name of the Lord our God, blessed is the name of our king! You are holy, righteous and worthy of honor. Yours is the majesty. Yours is the praise. Your name is highest in all the Earth.

Nothing compares to the scope of Your wisdom, plan, purpose, administration and execution of the cosmos. No one being could do what You do, to the extent that You do it, as well as You do it, or as completely as You do it. I exalt You, God, as ruler of and director of this boundless existence. You are creator, executor and builder of all that is and ever will be. You are the source of all input, all knowledge and all joy. You are the originator of love.

Thank You! Hallelujah to Your name! I am blessed to know that You love me! I appreciate You today and always! What do You want me to know today, Father?

**Day 39**

Father God,

You are an awesome God. I love You so much! You saved me, delivered me, kept me and still love me! What a mighty God You are. Thank You for being so incredibly awesome!

If all my life remains as it is now, I will still appreciate the grace You have given to me. Your mercy is new every day!

Today I pray for the women on my heart. I ask You to give them wisdom and to love them. Help them overcome the obstacles in their life and find You? Help them to see their need for You. Help them to deal with the life they have to live. Please do what is best for their family? Help them to find repentance. No one knows their need like You do. No one knows their pain like You do. Please love them? Be kind to their family, please? They are hurting and they need You today. Will You do whatever You can for them that is in their best interest?

Please help them in ways that I can't? I ask in Jesus' name. What do You want me to know today, Father?

**Day 40**

Father God,

You are incredible! Thank You for great thoughts! Thank You for allowing me to dream good dreams! Thank You for a vision that will enable me to bless people in need—especially those in need of You.

We all need You, God. More than life, more than living, and more than family, we need You! I rejoice to know You, my source, my savior, my provider, my joy! What a delight it is to be Your child! My heart rejoices in the love You have bestowed on me! My life is blessed to know that You have plans for my future and purpose for my life. As I see my friends struggle, please help them? Help them overcome their situations? In Jesus' name I ask these things.

As the song by Charles Gabriel says, "It is good to know, as I onward go, that the way of the cross leads home!"

I love You. Your heart is my comfort. Please help me hear Your heart? Help me to hear Your voice? I don't want to know anyone but You. I don't want to fail You. I don't want to hurt anyone. Please help me find my niche in life. What do You want me to know today, Father?

**Day 41**

Father God,

All the days of my life were spent at Your direction. All the events of my future will fulfill Your purpose for me. My life will somehow glorify You! You are beyond able! You are incomparably wonderful!

No one at anytime will ever compare to You. It gives joy to me to know that You love me. It's a great delight to be in Your sight. How can I ever please You? How can I be what You want me to be? Show me how to bless You? I've wasted so many years doing only what I want to do. How can I do what You want me to do? You are holy, wonderful, glorious, kind and pure. Your heart is so big and full of love. Your provision is so perfect. Your training methods are so awesome! You are complete and have every base covered. You amaze me! You delight me! You reward me by just listening to me! Beyond measure, beyond scope, You are beyond description, God. Originator of all substances and source of all supply, no one can do what You do! You impress me, God!

Thank You for all that You do for me. I love You! What do You want me to know today, Father?

**Day 42**

Father God,

Your purpose and plan are perfect. The execution of Your will is incredible. The complexity and compatibility of Your performance is awesome. You are so good, so true, so immeasurably intelligent! It blesses me to know that You have all our lives under control. Nothing, no one, no group of powers can be measured within distance of You because You are so superior.

It is my delight to be Your servant. It is my joy to be with You. Day in and day out I want to be in Your presence. I need to be with You. Your being encompasses the mere mortals I walk beside and am a part of daily. We are limited to form and substance. You have no limitations or boundaries. You have no restrictions. Doubt does not limit You. Lack of faith does not paralyze You. Your imagination is not based on pre-anything. If it has been done, it originated within the composite of Your being. Help me to grasp the scope of Your ability to work through me? Help me to walk in the fullness of all that You have planned for me. Help me to be more than I limit myself to be? I ask in Jesus' name. What do You want me to know today, Father?

**Day 43**

Father God,

I give my anger to You right now. I will not sit and rehearse my anger. I will not relive the events of today. What happened was not right and it should not have happened to me, but it did. But I refuse to commit it to memory. It was an event that is now history. I will not dwell on it. If I think on it, it will only make me bitterer. Help me to overcome my bitterness of the past? Help me overcome and forget my memories of all the wrongs that I have rehearsed and memorized?

I am a sinner as bad as he is. I will not let this event consume this day and be spoken of by me. I will not share the pain so I can place the blame. I will not tell the world what he did. I will not remember the slight or the consequences that will be with me all week. It is the little foxes that spoil the vines. I will not name this fox. It is trying to make me surrender my peace and steal the wonderful joy I have. I will not give it food. I will not give it opportunity to steal more from me.

Father, forgive me if I have wronged anyone? Forgive me if I have slighted anyone? Help me to be aware of what I do so I won't hurt them as I have been hurt? I ask in Jesus' name. What do You want me to know today, Father?

**Day 44**

Father God,

I was just working at the computer and realized that my inbox was trying to play a song at the same time as the media player. The result was an ugly conglomeration of a note here and a sound here. It made me wonder how many times my interruptions disrupt others and make them feel there is an ugly sound being made. I have such a hard time waiting for them to finish. I'm so sorry if my interruptions have disrupted their train of thought and caused them grief.

I haven't ever meant harm to others but they tell me I have hurt them. There isn't a mean bone in my body, but the presentation of my personality and nature has irritated and tried people to the utmost at times. I'm so sorry. If there is a way to rewrite my spoken output, would You fix me please? Would You redo my mental configuration so that I am pleasing to be around and a joy to know? I don't want to offend people but it just seems to happen.

Why is it that our own nature causes us so much trouble? Please forgive me for not bringing this to You sooner? I'm so stupid and selfish about these things. I ask You to do what You can with this old mess, in Jesus' name. What do You want me to know today, Father?

**Day 45**

Father God,

Some days I wish I couldn't identify with scripture so much. I awoke with another one of those dreams. It had to do with losing my job unfairly. And then the thought came to me that I had a Jericho Road experience. I was attacked, wounded and had been left for dead. The people who should have helped me then, didn't. They kept their distance and judged me. But You came along and loved me, treated me with compassion and rescued me. Thank You!

The ones who should have helped me the most, shot me with judgment! I once heard that Christians are the only people on the planet who shoot their own wounded. I never believed it was true, until I was the wounded one. Oh, how we hurt one another by judging them! No wonder the scripture says, "Judge not that ye be not judged" in Matthew 7:1.

And I realized in writing that to You that I have judged others. I have said and thought, "He or she shouldn't have done or said that". It was judgment! I have reaped in abundance now. But what grieves me the most now is the degree to which I have reaped. People always said, "Don't judge"; but they never said what judgment was. I never knew that it was deciding what someone should or should not have done. I can't possibly know their life and what You are doing in it. Forgive me? Help me never to do that to another human being? I beg of You, in Jesus' name, don't let me put anyone through what I've been through? What do You want me to know today, Father?

**Day 46**

Father God,

I am now and always will be grateful to You for Your faithfulness, consideration and help. You provide for me, keep me safe, and send me the work and the means to do it. You are divinely organized and completely structured and yet all that You do is creative and beautiful. I love to see the things You have put together and watch events manifest themselves as perfectly executed operations. You do what You do so well! And You do it to bless us because You love us so much when we deserve it so little. Thank You for the love, and the evidence that You have chosen to love us despite our unpleasantries. Thank You for the evident masterminding of our lives that allows us free will and yet brings us to complete fulfillment.

You are beyond description. Your capability overwhelms the human mind while intriguing us at the same time. How do You do what You do so well? Someday maybe I'll begin to comprehend the vastness of Your complexity and the beauty of Your intricacies.

I am now and forever will be impressed by You. Thank You for letting me have a peek at Your goodness and greatness to us. What do You want me to know today, Father?

**Day 47**

Father God,

It was incredible to know You today! I am blessed to know You and all that You are. Thank You for taking care of me and mine. Thank You for church! Magnificent Father, Holy Provider, Helpful Mentor. You are my hope and my future, God. Without You I have no hope for success in anything. Will You direct my path? No one understands what is good for us but You, God. Your wisdom surpasses our understanding. Your purpose far exceeds our concept of Your purpose for us. You are God! You rule! You overwhelm me with Your ability! Will You take care of my needs?

I need to know You more every day. Help me to be more like You, everyday? I love You and I need You. You are perfect in every way. Will You help me get control of my impulses? I am so in need of Your help. Will You give me some money so I can give some money? Will You give to worthy Christians? Will You bless excellent organizations?

Please do these things for me, in Jesus' name? What do You want me to know today, Father?

**Day 48**

Dear Father God,

Tomorrow is the anniversary of Mom's death. It has been 42 years since she died but it seems the time has gone so fast. She would be amazed and disappointed at where I am now. I've now lived longer than she did by years. I'm glad she didn't live to have some of the aches and pains I've had. I don't know why she completed her mission so quickly, but I know she succeeded with me, as far as anyone was able to do so. I am a force in a tiny box, as only You know. You knew me before she did. You placed me with her and Dad. You set me in the right place and the right time to train me for Your purpose. I often wonder why my life stays so challenging. I see people all around me that seem to have seamless flow of life with blessings all around, abundance of provision and comfort everywhere. Proverbs 22:2 says, "The rich and poor meet together: the LORD is the maker of them all." This scripture amazes me, but truth is truth and I thank You for giving me the life You decided was best for me.

Regardless of the events in my life, my future is not yet complete. I believe You are about to establish my purpose and begin to work through me to bless others. I ask You to release me into the full appointment that You have for me soon. Will You please initiate my purpose? Will You drop into place the final elements? You alone can release the final elements into place and reveal the vision for the mission You have for me. I ask in Jesus' name. What do You want me to know today, Father?

**Day 49**

Father God,

God, You alone are the Alpha and Omega. You begin and You end all things. You are always strong, always helpful, always wise and always present! I love You! I need You! You are so strong and so wise! Please help me get done all that You have given me to do? Help me accomplish what I have in front of me? You are able to help me. Will You? I need divine direction and help. You alone are perfect. You alone are the source of all truth and all wisdom. You rule with wisdom, glory and honor. Yours is the only name we can trust.

I am overwhelmed! I have to get moving! I'm so sorry. Please forgive me for what I didn't do that I should have done? You are so good to us! Thank You for Your mercy to my son. Please continue Your kindness to him? Please help him to be what You need him to be?

Thank You for helping me get this far. Thank You for letting me do the "what" I have gotten done. Please help me finish the job I have ahead of me? Please help me do all that You have called me to do. I rejoice that I know You and can trust in You! I ask for these things in Jesus' name. What do You want me to know today, Father?

**Day 50**

Father God,

You are almighty and full of power. You rule with dignity and power. You grant us mercy and grace everyday.

Thank You for sending me help with the cleaning. Please bless my helper? I appreciate her so much.

You have done so much for me and shown me so much mercy and grace; I appreciate You more every day.

Will You please help rebuild the lives of prisoners at the jail? Will You help them rebuild their own life? Will You heal them from their experiences? Will You give us wisdom as we speak to them?

Father, please help all prisoners everywhere to find You? Please send witnesses to the prisons who will teach them all truth and lead them into righteousness? Please do what is best for guards, prisoners, wardens, and all other officers? Please reform our system?

You are the wisest, the holiest, the greatest of all creations and the creator of all that is and ever will be. You are the founder, the originator and the resolver of all things. You expand us just by loving us. Please heed my requests, I ask in Jesus' name. What do You want me to know today, Father?

**Day 51**

Father God,

What an awesome God You are! You have no failures, no mistakes, nothing to regret. You are perfect in all things. I honor You, love You, and exalt You!

Your ways are higher than mine and Your purposes flawless. Your plan covers all the needs of all the people. Great and majestic is Your scheme. Your management skills overwhelm me!

I love You with all my heart, soul, mind and being. You are holy. You are righteous. You are true. You are far above all created beings and You are the source of all of them.

Powerful ruler and plentiful provider, You amaze us all with Your perfect provision. Thank You for Your generosity to me. Thank You for Your wisdom in keeping me humble and dependent on You.

You knew the path I would walk before I was born. You knew the destination before You sent me. Your purpose is my perfection. All-encompassing, all-knowing, always wise God, You astound me with Your grace and mercy.

I adore You. I worship You. You are my fulfillment and I delight to know You. What do You want me to know today, Father?

**Day 52**

Father God,

You are! Beyond all human reason, beyond human existence, God, You exceed life's most basic understandings. Your power is pervasive and immutable. Your grace is marvelous and immeasurable. No one can describe Your frame or comprehend Your existence. No one can define Your will. You and only You are capable of realigning a human life so that it brings You glory.

The issues of a human life are miniscule compared to Your ability to resolve them. We are so insignificant compared to the vast resources and forces at Your command. Truly, You are so good to us. Thank You for being so awesome. Thank You for forgiveness and mercy. We deserve so many penalties. Thank You for sparing us.

Multitudes will worship You without comprehending the scope of Your being. Millions will bow before Your throne in worship and only know that they love You! Many will seek Your grace instead of Your face. Please may I bask in Your love? May I be Your child? Today and everyday I need to be with You. I need to love You. I need to learn from You what love is. I love You. What do You want me to know today, Father?

**Day 53**

Father God,

You give the vision! You give the hope. I am a tool in Your hands. Use me.

Father, You are my only future. Without You, I can do nothing. I can't survive without Your love. I want to complete the plan You sent me to fulfill. Your truths are eternal and Your word is magnificent. Your promises are irrevocable. You are not capable of failure.

Oh, Father, I am looking forward to a new heaven and earth. They will come at the perfect time. Your purpose is perfect and holy. You are righteousness. You are love.

Morning by morning new mercies I see. Today and everyday, I exist at Your mercy. You are so patient and kind. Thank You for the love You give us and pour out upon us. Your gifts are eternal and help us to become Your likeness. You call is our job description. Your need is our response. We owe You our lives; our existence is dependent on Your good will. Thank You for planning our lives and allowing us to be in contact with You. When we converse with You, we know we are hearing from You and can serve You best.

Thank You for not revealing what it would be harmful for me to know. What do You want me to know today, Father?

**Day 54**

Father God,

Your word is awesome. No word spoken by You will return without fulfilling its mission. No one will fail to know You and see and recognize Your power.

You are love. Love is God working in me. I need You in me. I need Your power working in me. You are so good!

Help me, Father? Help me set aside my besetting sins? Help me to overcome my habits, iniquities, and death bringing behaviors? That which I allow to continue to be sin in me is killing me. Help me recognize and remove the sin?

Please, in Jesus' name, will You heal every Christian who is sicker than me now? Heal their pneumonias, illnesses, broken bones, open wounds, surgeries, and heartaches? Fix their lives so they bring glory to Your name?

Teach us, Father? Quickly give us all that we need to know in order to be all that we need to be.

Show me what I need to learn from You from this? And please help everyone who seeks Your face tonight? Let Your word go forth in speed and power and let Your purpose be fulfilled. What do You want me to know today, Father?

**Day 55**

Father God,

Marvelous! Marvagistic! Mavelous! Stupendous! Stupijestic! Encompariffic! Supervader! Invisibuffer! Superpowerific!

I just needed more adjectives to describe how great, marvelous, majestic, invincible, all-encompassing, compassionate, and powerful You are so I made some up! Language is too limiting!

From my heart to Your ears, I want You to know that every good thing that's ever been said about anyone could be said about You and it still wouldn't describe how much better You are than that.

Thank You for healing me! I can feel the improvement and I love You for it. Thank You for saving me. You gave Your greatest treasure so we could know Your greater love.

What it must have cost You I wish You Your equivalent of restful breezes, delightful music, sweet incense and delicious flavors. I hope You have sweet companionship, easy work, interesting challenges and someone to relax with. I hope You have babies' smiles, toddlers' giggles, children's laughter and teenage triumphs to watch. May You be blessed with comfortable seating, good armrests, pleasant views and a good listener for a friend.

Be at peace, God, be loved, be safe, You are needed! What do You want me to know today, Father?

**Day 56**

Father God,

Thank You for teaching me about giving! I love the fact that You are all about giving grace, mercy and forgiveness. You give so much more that we can give. You are too awesome! You rule.

Bountiful, beautiful, benevolent God, You are too far beyond what we are to describe.

You are kind and sweet, honest and true, giving and loving and always consistent. Oh, how I love You! Your love truly does reach to the heavens. Your love seeks no evil, speaks no hurt, and causes no harm. You are God.

Your being is so complex, loving, warming, delightful and precious. If I could use all the lists of all the great words ever spoken at the same time, I still could not express how good and great You are. You're incredible. You are beyond all that we ask or need. You are too much to comprehend.

I love all that You are, even the part that I can't understand. I love Your perfection of plan and completeness of purpose. I love Your delivery of our needs and Your mission of love. Thank You times ten billion for all You have done in my life! What do You want me to know today, Father?

**Day 57**

Father God,

You are awesome!

I love You! Thank You for such a great day!

You are so good to me! You have done so much for me. Thank You.

God, You are holy and wonderful and glorious. You touch my heart and fix my head and let me know You are so awesome! You rule with wisdom, glory and honor! You are incredibly wise. You know what I need and when I need it and why I need it! And You know all these things for everyone. It is so frustrating to know that I can't do anything to bless You! You deserve to be lauded and honored and praised! You deserve all the recognition and power and love we can give and more. You are in all ways and at all times perfect. You are a composite being of infinite complexity and extraordinary generosity. We grieve You daily and yet You love us and give us grace and mercy. The immensity of Your power, and the scope of Your ability overwhelms the mind and baffles the intellect. You are so awesome and so cool! I love You and I am totally dependent on Your grace and mercy. You are the only God and there is no substitute. What do You want me to know today, Father?

**Day 58**

Father God,

Awesome! Incredible! Wonderful! Beautiful! You are all these things and more. I depend on You. I rely on You. I need You!

In all ways and on all sides You are just and wise. Your intelligence enables Your purpose and You execute it with finesse. Your plan is perfect but our reception is so flawed. Only You could do what You do. To be a coordinator of galaxies is a feat only a perfect and loving God could begin to attempt and You are that God.

You know what is best for me and what is wisest for me. I trust You and I admit my own instability. I need You as my rock and my anchor. I need Your stabilizing influence in my life. I need You to help me through the mazes of deception and lies that have ensnared me and the ones I love. Show me Your truth? Help me to walk in wisdom and in humility? Help me to serve those You have called me to serve with love and kindness? In all ways and at all times, I am reliant on Your mercy and grace. Forgive me, Father, for I am a sinner and a fool? Help me and heal me; I need You more than life. I ask in Jesus' name. What do You want me to know today, Father?

**Day 59**

Father God,

U R 2 good 2 B 4 us. We R so needy of U. Will U B Rs 4 ever? We need U 2 B here now and everyday.

Thank You for allowing creativity! You are the creative creator of all creative and created beings. You love is so good and wise and pure. Thank You for being ever so kind and loving to us.

I bless the day You allowed me to be filled with Your Holy Spirit. It is Your spirit within me that causes me to be full of hope for the future. It is only my faith in You that lets me trust in Your provision and hope in Your promises. I love You with all my being. I need You and I need Your strength. I need Your direction to be confirmed to me. I need Your provision to be released to me.

In Jesus' name, I ask that You speak directly to me. I ask that You confirm Your call on me through others by word, prayer, and visions and dreams? Please set me up for success? I ask You to enlarge my borders and expand my opportunities for success in serving You? Please increase my witness, increase my knowledge and increase my ability to serve You. You can do all these things and I ask them for me in the authority of the name of Jesus. What do You want me to know today, Father?

**Day 60**

Father God,

You are so faithful and incredible. You are so good! I love You and I need You. Your purpose baffles me and bewilders me. Your plan is so unexplainable. You are without explanation or need for defense. You are so patient with me. Please help me to know Your plan for me? I need to know Your will and walk in obedience.

Show all of us what Your perfect will is and how we can fulfill it?

You are awesome and incredible. You amaze me with Your power and unending love. Your goodness and tranquility permeate our world. Your love is always faithful, true and dependable.

God, You are our source and our supplier. Your storehouse is never empty and Your supply is never meager. I rely on You without fear and without doubt.

My soul is a ship without a rudder without Your guidance. I need Your hand on my life and Your direction made clear to me. Help me to see Your guidance? I ask in Jesus' name. What do You want me to know today, Father?

**Day 61**

Father God,

Thank You for victory in life and death! You chose to spare me. I don't know why You have given me more time than others; I just know that I don't deserve to be here. I need a clue as to what to do next.

You are awesome and totally incredible. You rank higher than my imagination can reach for. You are the best of the best. Benevolent! Courageous! Faithful! You are all of these and more. You are our great and good and wonderful God! I adore You and appreciate You so much! You are wonderful.

Thank You for pets and gifts and love and kindness. You are the best giver and miracle worker I know. I can trust You with my future at all times. Thank You!

Tonight, will You bless all Christians who need to hear from You? Will You love and comfort all wounded saints?

Father, You are perfect in every way! Please meet my requests? I ask in Jesus' name. What do You want me to know today, Father?

**Day 62**

Father God,

You are too awesome! Your love is beyond my deepest imagination. Your purpose and plans are wiser than we can grasp. You are the designer, ruler and executor of our life. You coordinate and choreograph all the details of all the lives and it is a great comfort to know You are in control. You alone are capable of such a massive and awesome task. God, You astound the senses with Your majesty. You amaze the mind.

You are incredible and totally in charge. You impress me more every day in every way.

I love You and need You. Father, You bring me joy and comfort just to know You. You build me up and lead me in paths of righteousness. You are the director of my steps. You are the inspiration for my progress. I need You! I am totally dependent on You. You are an intelligent and comprehensive being whom we owe everything to. Without You, we are formless dust and empty vapors.

Almighty Creator—I want to see You and know You as You are. I want to be what You need me to be. I want to complete my part of Your plan. I love You, Father God. What do You want me to know today, Father?

**Day 63**

Father God,

You are the ultimate leader. You are invisible, unavoidable, irresistible, and uncontainable. You are trustworthy, excellent, awesome and magnificent. You are before the beginning and after the end of all things. You are the pre-existent, all-empowering, all-encompassing royal and glorious creator. You give me life, hope, joy and comfort. You enable me, astound me, enrich me and uplift me. You give me rest, power and courage. You are my only future. You are unlimited, unhindered, and unhampered in any way. If I spent all my life working for You I would still not repay You for all You have done for me.

I need You this morning and every morning. I need Your love, Your comfort Your courage and Your direction. I need Your plan and direction for my life. I need Your hope.

Father, we can not live without Your mercy. Thank You for new mercies every morning! Thank You for new grace. You are a faithful and just God. You are wonderful!

You impress me, amaze me and blow me out of the water! You are so good and so precious, You are just not qualifiable! Thank You, God! What do You want me to know today, Father?

**Day 64**

Father God,

Im-pressive! Glo-rious! Mag-ni-fi-cent! You are awe-some! You are stupendous! In all things and at all times, You are overwhelmingly superior! Yours is an all-encompassing love that supersedes the imagination. Your being is so complex, so perfect, so wonderful that it can't be described. You are the destination of my heart.

Father, You alone can comfort me. You set my life in order and align my will to Yours. You direct my steps and give me strength to continue. You feed and guide and train me while You provide for me and all of us.

My existence is dependent on Your mercy and Your grace. My purpose is but a cell in the elbow of Your arm. By Your grace, I live to function as You will, although I stumble and balk at every step.

Forgive me for my stubbornness, please? Help me to be pliant and yielded to You? Break me and my will, Father. Cause me to do Your will and only Your will. Cause me to do Your will Your way.

No one can please You in their own strength. We all need to lean on Your wisdom, Your strength, Your knowledge. Help all of us to turn off our will and turn on obedience? Help me???!! I choose obedience and You! And I ask for Your help in Jesus' name. What do You want me to know today, Father?

**Day 65**

Father God,

Thank You for confirming Your work in me. Thank You for completing Your work in me. Thank You for bringing me into alignment with Your purpose for me.

You are able, bountiful, creative, defining, earnest, fearless, gracious, helpful, ingenious, just, kind, life-giving, majestic, nice, open, powerful, quintessential, renewed, sturdy, trustworthy, understanding, victorious, and wise.

Beyond our goals and before our dreams, You exist. Aware of our limitations and sure of our destinations, You exist. Provider of our present and source of our future, You exist. You are, have been, will be and will have been all the days of my life. You contain our substance.

Father of all creations, giver of our redemption, director of our growth, You are generous and good, blessing and giving life to all.

Blessed is Your name. Holy, holy, holy You are. Wonderful, loving, good and faithful, You are our final stop.

You are my hope, my future and my anchor for the present.

I have joy in knowing You. You are my life, my lifeline and my life current. I love You. What do You want me to know today, Father?

**Day 66**

Father God,

You are so awesome! I'm impressed by all that You do and all that You are! You overwhelm me with Your love, mercy, grace and kindness. You are always faithful and always wise.

I love You and appreciate You. I need You and I miss You.

Incredible God! Impressive and all creative Father, You are so purposeful. You are in all ways and all times holy and perfect.

Total and comprehensive, ready and attentive, You rule with wisdom in glory. Your imagination is incomparable. Your purpose is perfect. Our future is in Your hands. Our plans are foolishness and folly in Your eyes and we are worthless without You. We are helpless without You. Our hopes are a waste of time and our goals are a diversion of the enemy without Your leadership.

You are magnificent and marvelous. You are comforting and reliable.

I can't think, breathe, walk or talk without You. Oh, how I need You! I need Your direction, Your wisdom, Your light and Your plan. Please direct me? Advise me? Push me where I need to go? Please help me do what will please You? Please help me do well what needs doing? I ask in Jesus' name. What do You want me to know today, Father?

**Day 67**

Father God,

Precious, awesome, glorious, God. You are my source and my joy. I love You and adore You! You are totally incredible and worthy of love and adoration. You are completely whole and comprehensively active. I love You! I need You! I want to be with You.

God, You are forever kind and good to me. Thank You for my great family and Your gracious love.

You are able to strengthen me and keep me well and whole. You are able to surround us with a great cloud of witnesses to Your perfect plan and perfect purpose. Let me love You forever? Let me hold You and hope in Your forever? You are my only consolation and my only salvation. You keep me safe and protect me from all attacks and attackers from Satan. You have taught me and blessed me and kept me safe and whole. You have brought me to a place of servitude where I can be of value to You. You may have my soul, my spirit, and my body for Your use and Your glory.

Thank You, Father, for all that You have done, are doing and will do for me. Please grant my requests? I ask in Jesus' name. What do You want me to know today, Father?

**Day 68**

Father God,

You are the wisest of the wise. You have done all that You can in the best possible way. You are the best and You give the best. Thank You!

You are the one I trust and love. You are the keeper of my heart. You enrich me and bless me. You increase me. You do all things because You are perfect and wise.

God, You are so strong and powerful. You are so wise and overcoming. I love You for all that You do!

God of creation and King of all Kings, God of all forms of life, You are holy. Righteousness, peace and joy are Your trademark signatures.

You grant to us all the things we need and want as we stay in Your will. I praise You. I praise You for Your perfection, Your abundance and Your timing.

All is perfect and well in You—it gives me hope to know that. What do You want me to know today, Father?

**Day 69**

Father God,

You are awesome beyond degree! You surpass the mind's ability to imagine Your capability. You exceed the limitations of description. You are overwhelmingly impressive. Oh, how I love You! Oh, how I want to be with You.

You are so cool! I love You!

Thank You for all that You have done and are doing for me! And thank You for adjusting me!

Oh, hallelujah! You rule! You reign in majesty and power and glory and honor! I appreciate You! I reverence You! I honor You because You are so good and so wise!

I will never know or discover any being as complex and as perfect as You!

Thank You!

Honoring and obeying You is the only thing I must do. You have ordered my steps and are directing my paths!

Holy, holy, holy, Lord God Almighty, full of power, grace, mercy and holiness; I adore You!

Father of the fatherless and home builder for the poor, You bless me, day in and day out! What do You want me to know today, Father?

**Day 70**

Father God,

You are my source and my joy! You are the one I love and need above all things. Please, please, hold me? I want to move on to the next level. I want to make progress in You!

You are my reason for being here. I love You so much.

I want to be a completely compliant and willing slave. I want to be Your arm extended to the hurting. We are all disappointments to You; we are all failures. Oh, I am so sorry. You have made us to be Your companions and yet we have so little time for You. I am so sorry that I have failed You so many times. I can't imagine what You must feel to know that those You loved the most rejected You. I can't imagine how much it must hurt You.

You are so good and so wonderful. You are precious and loving and always forgiving. You are the best friend I've ever had. You are the only friend I can fully trust. You are my hero, my comfort and my hope.

I love You, Father. I need You now and everyday!

Thank You for loving me as only You can? What do You want me to know today, Father?

**Day 71**

Father God,

Nobody helps me like You do, Father. Nobody is there for me like You are! I love You and I admire and appreciate You. You are my only dependable friend. I worship You. I adore You. You are all powerful, always capable, and everlastingly wonderful.

Awesome God! You are beyond definition. I need You! I love You. Wise and wonderful Father; You are my source for all things. You're my hero and my hope and future.

You restore my soul and make me walk in paths of righteousness. I love You, holy, powerful, confident and commanding one! Glorious in purpose and plan, You are incomparable and unrestricted. Caring and compassionate, You embrace me with an eternal love.

Goodness and kindness are Your mode of operation. You love us to life and bless us to fulfillment.

Impressive in glory, immensely strong, indescribably good, and eternally gracious to me, You are my future and my destination.

Oh Father, teach me Your will? Please, help me walk and live in Your will? I ask it in Jesus' name. What do You want me to know today, Father?

**Day 72**

Father God,

Always faithful and ever my guide, You are my anchor and the chain that holds me fast. I am safe in Your arms and dependent on Your power. I love You; You are mine and mine alone! I can rely on You, depend on You, lean on You and You will never fail me. Always and evermore, Your love will be a consistent and continuous force for change and my betterment. You are perfect and are perfecting me. Out of Your wisdom You have directed the steps of my life. You have established a path for me to walk in and a future that will glorify You! How wonderful is Your name and Your presence! I rely on Your sweetness and Your compassion! I depend on Your mercy and grace. No one at any time can begin to compare with any aspect of Your ability.

Because of You, I can be righteous, love others, and live without shame. You are gracious and all encompassing. I will love You all the days of my life and strive to serve You with all of my heart. In Jesus' name, I ask You to bless me. What do You want me to know today, Father?

**Day 73**

Father God,

My sweet, sweet Father, I love You so much! Thank You for keeping my family safe thus far. Thank You for the possibility of work. Thank You for loving me although I don't deserve it. Thank You for Your continuous grace and mercy on my life.

You are wise. You are powerful and yet so kind. You love with an everlasting love. Your touch is evident in the entire world. Your life is omnipresent all around. Your Spirit is within me. You are the One. The only God, ever-faithful, ever-listening, ever-generous; You are my heart's desire. You envelope us in love day-in and day-out. How I love You! Thank You for letting me come to know You better day and night.

I rejoice in the changes You have wrought in my life. You have given me life eternal and I am so unworthy. You saved me by the blood of Your Son, Jesus. He has rescued me from the tormentor. Thank You for Jesus. It is joy unspeakable and full of glory to know You and worship You, Father. Hallelujah, my Father! Holy, holy, holy, holy is Your name forever, from everlasting to everlasting. What do You want me to know today, Father?

**Day 74**

Father God,

Thank You for working in my home and in me tonight. Thank You for working on us!

You are so bountiful! You are massive! Father, You bless without reason, teach for our enrichment and love me!

Thank You! You rule! You are not confined in any way or limited by any boundaries. Still, You have time for me. Thank You!
Be blessed! Be rewarded! You are so worthy! You are so very good!

I love You and need You so much! You are my strength. You are my only strength. You continue to let me live when I deserve termination.

Holy! Holy! Holy! Lord God Almighty! You are worthy to be loved and adored! You are indescribably great and marvelous. It frustrates me to be unable to say the full extent of Your love. You supersede language, syntax and description!

Beautiful, extensive, delightful, Father! I rejoice that You love me! It gives me great strength to know You have noticed me.

Hallelujah! You rule! You are so good! I adore You!

Father, I love You! What do You want me to know today, Father?!

**Day 75**

Father God,

Thank You for letting me have friends for all these years. Many have been such a blessing to my life. Thank You for all the blessings You have given me in friends. Even the ones who have been true friends and have spoken painful truths to me have been good. Some have done what others wouldn't. Thank You for continuing Your work on me.

You are my best friend and my forever friend! You tell me the truth to help me! You love me to life. Thank You for being all that I need and want. You are so wonderful to me!

Because You are my hope, I can go on. Thank You for not giving me that job! Thank You for being my future. Thank You for letting me live on the privileged planet!

Your wisdom and Your plan are so vast, so incomprehensible in scope, that it blows away all the boundaries of the mind. What an amazing person You must be! You are our amazing deity. I don't know how You came to be but I am so glad that You came to be! I'm full of joy at the thought that someday I may actually get to be in the sea around Your throne! Until then, I do now, and always will, love You. What do You want me to know today, Father?

**Day 76**

Father God,

Thank You for letting me be the recorder of Your poem today! Thank You for a creative, encouraging and hopeful word.

My efforts are so puny when I try to worship You with my puny little talent. You deserve the accolades of billions. You are worthy of the adoration of all living things. You are all good things. You are all my hope and all I will ever need.

Provider, inspirer, designer, director, diviner, discerner—all these and more—You are God!

Eternal, immortal, forever Father, Your breath is the air I breathe. Your mercy extends the seconds of my life. Your grace continues my heartbeat! You love enriches me. Your provision enables me.

Minute by minute I lose my life. Day by day I miss the mark. Year by year I've spent on me. Oh, forgive me, Father? Change me? Redeem the minutes? Buy back the years? Help me bring glory to Your name?

Thank You for Your goodness to me!

If I could make a way or find the secret I would bless You. I can't think of a single thing that You didn't give me. I can only set my purpose to love You and that I do, because You are so worth it. What do You want me to know today, Father?

**Day 77**

Father God,

You are Father. My source, my joy, my hope, my future and my forever, I love You!

Eternal, immortal, invisible, irresistible, uncontrollable, marvelous and mighty, I love You!

Unique, indivisible, unlimited, unbound, understated, and untied, I love You!

Delightful, deliberate, desirable, designed, defined, indescribable and deity, I love You!

Glorious, grand, great, generous, genuine, good, and grounded, I love You!

Marvelous, majestic, missioned, mindful, melodious, and mighty, I love You!

Faithful, fabulous, fearful, finished, final, founded, far reaching and fair, I love You!

Caring, careful, cautious, creative, customized to love, caring, and curing, I love You!

Blessed, beautiful, bountiful, boundless, bare, bearing, beloved, and burdenless, I love You! What do You want me to know today, Father?

**Day 78**

Father God,

Because of You I can face whatever comes my way. Jesus came and You allowed him to pay the price of my pain and it gives me joy to know that He did it. Thank You for the love You gave! Thank You for Your mercy that keeps You from giving me what I truly deserve. Thank You for the grace that spared this sorry human.

Always wise and careful, Father, You are my guide, my comfort and my hope. You dwell in me to direct my every step.

My mind can't comprehend what my heart tells me—that You are God. You came to us as Jesus, and You dwell in me. In me You can do anything. You have all power. You are master of the universe. You are able to do whatever You need done. You will work through me despite all opposition. You are able. I am a willing vessel. Take my shell and use it to Your glory! Let Your work and Your name be glorified. Father, You rule, You reign, and You are so wise. What do You want me to know today, Father?

**Day 79**

Father God,

The sound of Your name is so glorious! Your plan and purpose are flawless!

Wonderful Father! Glorious Lord! Your name is all powerful! Your name is full of authority! Your name is boundless and all encompassing! Hallelujah! You are marvelous beyond description. You are beautiful beyond compare. I surrender all that I am and ever want to be to You. Holiness belongs to You. All righteousness is Yours. No one can compare with Your love and Your mercy! Great and mighty is Your name of names. Great and mighty is God. Holy, powerful and full of truth, Your love is my delight. You are wonderful and beautiful in every way.

Thank You for being my father. Thank You for loving me. Thank You for helping me. I bless Your name and rejoice to know You! I am so glad You are my father.

Awesome, wonderful, king God, You are so blessed. You bless me everyday in every way! How wonderful You are! Thank You for being so very good to me today! You are wise, cautious, careful, caring, delightful, desirous, elegant, extremely good, and perfect in every way.

I love You so much! Thank You for being there for me in every way!

I appreciate You and Your patience, Father; You are my anchor in every storm. Thank You for being my home and my helper. Thank You for being all that You are. What do You want me to know today, Father?

**Day 80**

Father God,

Dearest of all, I wish I were home with You! I wish we had a day of sweet fellowship.

You are so good to me. You are so precious and so faithful. I love to know You and know that You will never fail me. You are my hope and my future.

You are so wonderful and wise, Father. You are perfect in every way. You fulfill me as no one else can. You sustain me as no one else can. Thank You! You are honorable in all that You do. Thank You!

You are worthy of all love, power, glory and adoration! Wonderful, gracious, awesome God; holy, holy, holy is Your name! I bless Your name. I praise Your name! Yahweh! God of Heaven and Earth! I bless Your plan and purpose, since it is perfect. Wonderful name, glorious name, beautiful, perfect name of God, You are my hope. Holy name! Sanctified name! I love You! You are perfect. Your name is perfect. Your description is perfect. Most blessed of all, best of all beings, Father, You are so wise and perfect; no one can touch You for power, love, mercy or grace.

We all need You! We all desire You! We all pursue Your love! Great is Your name and worthy of all honor and praise. Glorious, wonderful, powerful name. Majestic, purposeful, authoritarian name.

Father, provider, lover, giver, sustainer, You're all of these, God. Thank You. What do You want me to know today, Father?

**Day 81**

Father God,

I need You so much! I am so alone without You. I have no one who
meets my needs like You do. No one cares for me and keeps me like You do.
You are so wonderful to me. You are always good and always wise.

Ever loving, never failing, perfect Father, I love You. Beyond my family,
beyond my connections, before my goals, You exist as my only hope. You are
my only consolation. In all of life's frustrations and failures, You remain
infallible. You stand unmovable, my tower in time of need. My heart is tied to
Yours. My life is connected to You. My only joy is in You. You meet my
needs when all others fail me. You are my rest and my restoration.

I need You. I want You. Let me be with You always? Let me be Yours?
Please don't keep me from Your presence? Let me be with You all of my time
and all of my life? No one meets me and cares for me like You do. No one will
ever be good to me. No one loves me like You do. Please don't keep me from
You? Never shut me out of Your heart? I ask in Jesus' name. What do You
want me to know today, Father?

**Day 82**

Father God,

Wonderful! Marvelous!

You exceed our dimensions and supersede our existence. You encompass our plane and define our limitations.

Before the extent of the universe, You lived. Before the first cell was even made, You loved. Before the first breath was taken, You created. Glorious and full of power, You are beyond mere descriptions of beauty. You are before all, in all, through all and after all things.

We imitate You in every move we make, every step we take and continuously fall short of Your glory.

How can I not love You? How can I not serve You? How may I be of service to You?

I love You! I need You! I am desperate for You. Father, You alone can still my trembling. You alone can stop my pain. You alone can keep me when all around me is sinking sand.

You are the net for my cliffs. You are the bridge over my troubled water. You are my shelter from the storm. Please don't push me away? What do You want me to know today, Father?

**Day 83**

Father God,

Amazing provider! You are so awesome. I am convinced that You alone are able to met my needs and be trusted.

You touch my heart and reach me when no one else can. I love You. I know You are creative and capable. You keep me safe and strengthen me when I am weak. Wonderful, loving, considerate, You are higher than all. No one protects us and cares for us like You do. No one keeps our love and never violates our trust like You do.

Wise and compassionate, You dole out our provision just as we need it. Thank You! Thank You for not giving us enough to get us in trouble. Thank You for entrusting us with so much. Great generous benefactor, we rely on You because You never fail us.

Holy, holy, holy, Lord God Almighty. You are our source and our storehouse. Wonderful keeper of my heart, I love You!

Bountiful and beautiful, You encourage me by Your presence. It is good to know that You care for me so much when I am so small in Your eyes. Thank You! What do You want me to know today, Father?

**Day 84**

Father God,

You are my hope! All the days of my life, I look to the day when I will see Your glory fulfilled. Thank You for letting Jesus come and complete Your plan for my redemption. Before Jesus came into my life, I was without hope, without future and wandering aimlessly. Having Your purpose as my goal gives me hope for a future without pain, suffering, or sorrow. Having You as my hope gives me joy and delight. You will never fail me. You will never let me down. You will never disappoint me.

Heart of all hearts, You are the greatest love of all. You are the best of all things at all times.

Creator of the future, You know our resolution. You can be trusted with all we hope and long for. You can be entrusted with the loves of our hearts. Because You are beyond limitation, we can rest in our present and trust in our future.

You are my security. You are my completion! Royal encompasser, You are in full control, absolute in power and full possessor of knowledge. You are my all. What do You want me to know today, Father?

**Day 85**

Father God,

Before You created time, You were the I am.

Before You created days and nights and season, You were.

Before there was air or water or earth, You lived.

Before there was power or weakness, You ruled.

Before the first breath, the first sound, the first pain or first loss, You
loved.

And You remain the creator.

You remain the regulator of seasons.

You remain the giver of ALL THINGS.

And You are the comforter and consoler of all hurting beings.

In light of Your power, Your load and Your scope of capability, I am a
dust mite on the planet. What joy it is to know that You created me to commune
with You! What joy it is to talk to You about all my days! You will always be
there for me. You will never tire of my weaknesses. I choose to be with You,
Father, You are my ever-after friend! Divine delight, I am blessed to know that
You care so much for me and about me. Until next time…What do you want
me to know today, Father?

**Day 86**

Father God,

When I have sinned, I am naked before You. I am without defense for I have wounded the one who loves me most.

I am dirt in a shell without Your forgiveness. Please don't turn away? Please forgive me? Please let me know Your love? I acknowledge that I am a failure. Without You I can't breathe. Every time I take a breath I am living as Your creation for Your glory. How can I fail You? How can I allow myself to fail such perfect and all encompassing love?

I test Your love with my foolishness, and try Your patience with ugliness. My sins rise before me and stand as a testimony to my limitations in light of Your mercy. Merciful Father, I walk in Your grace; I'm reminded of Your love daily. I don't deserve Your love or forgiveness. I don't deserve Your mercy.

Thank You for listening. Thank You for loving me and keeping me. Thank You for letting me live and for loving me.

Wonderful, wonderful, holy God, all power is Yours. You are the one true lover of my soul. What do You want me to know today, Father?

**Day 87**

Father God,

No one sees You or talks with You face to face. We are made in Your image and are multi-faceted. I can't imagine the complexity of Your being. I can't conceive of a being with Your comprehensibility.

Your existence is baffling to the limitations of my mind. Yet I know that it is the fact that I can't understand or comprehend You in any way that makes You worthy of all my love and devotions.

I do adore You! My excellent haven, You provide a place of rest and comfort that no one can take from me! You give me shelter and a hiding place from all of life's storms. You are my fortress, my protector and my covering. Behold, I am totally dependent on You! I am living in Your shadow; under Your wings is my refuge. I trust in Your buttresses. I lean on Your reinforcements.

I am weak where You are strong. Your power is greater than the sum of all other powers. All the energy in the world is not equivalent to Your force of being. How great You are! What do You want me to know today, Father?

**Day 88**

Father God,

Precious beyond expression, You are the love of my heart. You are the keeper of my heart. Precious key holder, how can I ever express to You my gratefulness? How can I communicate my desire to give You joy?

I am bound and gagged when I try to write what I feel for You. My pen can't write what my heart feels.

Your love fills me with joy. You enrich me and overflow my heart with Your goodness.

Oh, that I could find the words to say back a tiny portion of what I feel in response to Your endless perfect love.

Father of perfection, Your love urges me to holiness. Your love pulls me to righteousness. I am drawn to goodness and truth as I spend time with You. Glorious creator, You present me with endless opportunities to serve. Let me serve You in fullness of joy? Help me find ways to be Your voice to a hurting world. Help me find ways to communicate Your love to the most wounded? I ask in Jesus' name. What do You want me to know today, Father?

**Day 89**

Father God,

I have so much to thank You for today. You have spared the ones I love the most, and done the most for those who deserve the least!

You love is so forgiving! Thank You for not keeping score. Thank You for never saying, "I told You so."

Your love overlooks our faults and forgets our habits and cleanses our sins! How great is Your love! You are so perfect!

Wonderful, kind and caring Father, I don't deserve to know You. I am so unworthy of Your love. Please forgive me for all the stupid, lazy, mean things I do? Please help me to stop doing them?

Incredible, unrestricted, unlimited Father, You are so great! You are forever love. You are my security, my anchor, my wonder. Oh, how I love being with You!

I love to be near You. I love to be with You! I love to know that as much as I love You, You love me a thousand times more.

You are so much more precious than life itself. I appreciate Your goodness and love to me!

Thank You for all that You are, all that You do and for being there for me. What do You want me to know today, Father?!

**Day 90**

Father God,

Thank You for the blessing of this day! Thank You for reminding me that there is a hell. Thank You for reminding me that I am saved from a terrible and unceasing torture. Thank You for coming to us as Jesus and dying a horrendous death for us.

I am not worth the great sacrifice You made. You have loved the unlovely and forgiven the unforgivable. You are the transcender of space, time, distance and barriers. You have come to do what I could not; You have come to claim us as Your chosen. Thank You for choosing me! Your least worthy child, I appreciate You for all You did and are still doing.

It is so good to know that the wisest of all is in control. Your vision includes the invisible and comprehends the confusion. You set aside our objections and futile arguments. It is Your goodness that lets us learn one day at a time. It is Your love that lets us grow from all events.

Our troubles bless us as we learn to overcome them. Thank Your for letting us experience You in the midst of our pain. I love You and I'm learning to appreciate You so much more every day. What do You want me to know today, Father?

**Day 91**

Beloved Father,

Every thought of You makes me smile. Your goodness is amazing. Your solutions are perfect, timely, and always appropriate! What a joy to watch You work! In every situation You include and exclude just the right elements to bring life and growth. Hallelujah!

To walk in Your path is an adventure in amazement. To see the work of Your hands is to watch a master craftsman. Marvelous to see and delightful to participate in, I love Your walk!

To be part of Your plan is to see the orchestration of millions of components, coming together perfectly and seamlessly! It is as if the universe is a huge body with each part moving in total synchronization and nanosecond timing, with every minute particle falling in step at exactly the right moment in time. The beauty of the interaction is that it all seems so effortless to You!

Complex simplicity in translucent formulation, it is a reward to behold You, Father!

Delightful choreographer, You are music in motion. I love to watch Your composition! What do You want me to know today, Father?

**Day 92**

Father God,

Your have a perfect home planned for me. Thank You! I will spend eternity in Your house. It's more than I can imagine.

How great is Your love that You would allow us to share Your space! You alone have the power to place us and assign us our final work. Yet You promise us dwelling places on streets of gold on a level of grandeur that we can't imagine.. We don't deserve even shacks in the woods, but Your word describes gold and precious stones. How good it is to know You are the master builder. Your homes are perfect, flawless and specifically designed for each individual.

How foolish we are to think we own anything. The earth is Yours and all that is in it. We are comedians if we believe we can claim any rights to any of it. Thank You for allowing us to claim ownership of our meager possessions. It is dust claiming dirt and still gives us great pride. We are silly to believe we can do anything or own anything. I can almost see You chuckle at those who believe they have great possessions.

All that I have is Yours, Father. I'm sorry if I've claimed to own it. Please forgive me for doing what I want with my temporary area of imaginary "ownership" of Your kingdom? I ask in Jesus' name. What do You want me to know today, Father?

**Day 93**

Father God,

You are so grounded! I appreciate Your solid foundation. My life is safely built on the truths of Your kingdom. You love upholds me. Your power strengthens me. Your Holy Spirit cleanses me and teaches me.

I love You! I love to know You! I love to be with You. Everyday I choose You again, because You never fail me. You never let me down. You never blame me. You will never hold me accountable for the sins of my past if I confess them and ask forgiveness. Please help me live so that on judgment day, my life for You will have been exemplary? I know that You expect me to express Your heart and voice to this world. Please help me to do that?

You know that it is my own free will that leads my rebellions. I am in my own way. I set my will to do Your will and then fail us over and over again. At this point I have no excuses. But I ask in Jesus' name that You forgive me again and help me again? And in Jesus' name I choose by an act of my will to do Your will! I attach my will to the will and purposes of Your kingdom. Help me to keep myself in line? Help me mind my will? I ask in Jesus' name. What do You want me to know today, Father?

**Day 94**

Father God,

We are the pieces in your puzzle. We compose Your picture to the world. I'm so sorry there are pieces that are not in their place. Please help me get to my placement? I don't want to live life as it is now: I don't fit here. I want to be where my edges interact to bring completion and life to those around me. I know that my spirit was created by You and it is whole and beautiful because You don't do less than perfection. But I sense that I'm misplaced somehow. My spirit has been dis-eased and it longs for a homework assignment to fulfill. Help me home-in to where I fit?

A good sewing machine can help the operator make beautiful things, especially if it "comes home" well. The homing mechanism indicates perfect balance of operation as it works and then rests at just the right place. I want to be that machine in Your hands. Help me find the balance I need? Help me hone my parts until they work together without burrs or missed teeth? Help me help You do beautiful work?

I ask in Jesus' name, please? What do You want me to know today, Father?

**Day 95**

Father God,

I love You for the day when I can be with You and Jesus. I want to look into Your eyes and tell You both how much I appreciate all Your help and sacrifices.

You are worthy of all my praise! All that I endure is nothing compared to knowing that You have prepared a better place for me. My life is temporary here and I long to begin eternity in a better place.

We are such a mess here below. Each of us does what seems good to us and we are like a batch of balls in an air chute. Everyone bouncing around and nobody accomplishing anything. It must be hilarious to watch sometimes! Each of us says, "I'm the best ball." Then "No, I'm the best". All of us claiming to be on top then realizing we are on the bottom. Foolishness reigns in us. We don't consider that we are but shaped dust. Like sand castles doomed by the next wave, we are stacks of pride and goals that will end in a second.

You are the only worthy purpose in our life. You are the only destination that matters. Help me focus on Your purpose and become a ball bearing in Your machine? I'm tired of being a circus ball. I ask in Jesus' name. What do You want me to know today, Father?

**Day 96**

Father God,

What is my function?  If I could choose, I would be one of these:

If I were part of a car, I'd be the brake, saving people from danger.

If I were part of a ship, I'd be the lookout, watching the sea ahead.

If I were part of a house, I'd be the door lock, fastened against evil.

If I were part of an orchestra, I'd be the trumpet, proclaiming Your word.

If I were part of a lamp, I'd be the wick, carrying Your oil to the flame.

If I were part of a lighthouse, I'd be the machine that keeps the light turning and enabling the light to guide and protect.

My nature is to be the steering wheel, but I lack wisdom about directions. I'd be the ship captain, but I lack knowledge of the sea.  I'd be the door, but I would let in the enemy.  I'd be the orchestra conductor but I can't hear the music in my heart.  I'd be the flame, but I could never trust someone else to do the wick and would have to try alone and would soon go out.  I'd be the light, but my pride would be too much for the equipment to bear.

Am I truly just a bumper, destined to be hit?  Am I a dump valve on a ship, a door mat, a pit rag, or the charcoal of the lamps?  Show me my place, Father? I trust You to place me where I can truly be of the most use.  I ask in Jesus' name. What do You want me to know today, Father?

**Day 97**

Father God,

Thank You for progress in my life! Thank You for moving things that were immovable. You are supreme! You can do anything and You always do what is best for all of us. It befuddles me to try to figure out how You do that so I give up. But I will never give up telling You how neat it is that You can do that! Go God! Do what You do! You blow me away with Your ability to pull all of our "its" off! Just to see what You do for just me is mind-blowing! Then to multiply that a bazillion times is "like wow" to quote my younger friends. You put the "wow" in every day and You do it with flair!

You mix a batch of humans like a big bowl of dough and somehow combine this mess of fruits and nuts into the best fruitcake ever made. Nobody born on this planet can match Your ability. We are proud when we can get children to play together. You get us to work together! And the result is testimony to Your goodness and majesty.

Oh, how I love You! You are so good! You are so impressive! Aaah! I can't find words to tell You how cool You are! You know! What do You want me to know today, Father?

**Day 98**

Father God,

From the day I was created, You knew I would be where I am today. Your mind knew the thoughts of my heart and still You turned me loose to grow and learn. How often I must fail You and grieve You. I feel like Your biggest disappointment often. I am so sorry. My sins rise up before You. Please forgive me of all my sins?

I give up so easily. Every speed bump rises like a wall and I stop to pay homage to it. I should spit on it and look forward to the goal. Things a child would step over and giggle at consume my attention. I need to conquer my thoughts. I need to renew my mind and order my conversation.

Give me a way and a means to harness these thoughts. Cleanse my mind? Help me fill it with good and pure thoughts?

I've lived in a land that embraces perversity. I have absorbed the sins of my peers. I have taken in their misplaced focus, human reasoning and ungodly practices. Please cleanse me of these things? I need Your help, Father. Please set me free? I ask in Jesus' name. What do You want me to know today, Father?

**Day 99**

Father God,

What a glorious day You have made! I know that somewhere there is rain but I am so glad that You provided a glorious day this holiday. Thank You for making it safe for the holiday travelers. I makes me wonder if someone prayed for such a day today. I wish I could thank them. Thank You for answering their prayer! You must hear millions of prayer requests daily. Do You have a processing center where angels weed them out and stamp them "approved" or "disapproved" or "dump the blessing truck on this one"? Do You have a heavenly stamp pad that includes "not yet" or "no, not my will"? Is there a stamp that says "absolutely" or one that is a checklist of yes or no on each part of the prayer? Are the angels lined up waiting to run and follow Your instructions? Do Your head angels weed out the obvious "no" answers before You see them? And do they send the obvious yes answers and simply stamp the request "done" for You to see? Does Jesus hand You some that are marked, "Mine, please do this?" or "Okay by me"? I know You can't say no to those, You're his dad. Oh, it's good to know You are. I'd love to see the heavenly chain of command someday. Until next time, I love You. What do You want me to know today, Father?

**Day 100**

Father God,

I'm thinking of praying but I know that to get a definite yes, I have to pray Your will. What are the tests for Your will? Help me think on paper...

Is the prayer scriptural?

Is it godly love speaking?

Is it selfish?

Is it in the best interest of all concerned?

Does it look good and sound good but You can see that it isn't good?

Did the Holy Spirit pray it through someone?

Is it for someone's bodily healing?

Is it for someone's spirit to be healed?

Will it help the person be what You need them to be?

Does it violate free will?

Is it manipulative?

Father, this leaves me with one prayer today. Will You please, in Jesus' name, and in Your wisdom, do what is best for me and for those I love?

I don't want to put any limits based on my limited understanding.

Out of Your goodness, Your supply and Your storehouse, will You answer this prayer, please? What do You want me to know today, Father?

**Day 101**

Father God,

We remember the fallen but yet they must fall. Your word tells us that the number of martyrs must be fulfilled. Thousands will die for their faith and ten thousands will mourn them. Each one will leave a lasting testimony that their commitment was worth dying for.

Prepare me, Father. When the day comes when I must pass the test, let me be ready to stand firm in my faith? Give me the backbone to say how much I love You and how much You are worth to me.

Help me find ways to witness? Help me to share the truth of Your kingdom? My days are full of emptiness and chasing the wind. I live to follow my nose and it is a pathetic existence. I insist on my own way and my own needs being met and it shames me to write it.

My redemption was paid for with blood and I can't even tell a neighbor. I want to stand before thousands and yet can't speak up to one. How deceived I am to think that I am anything.

Why do You spare me? Why do You allow me my foolishness? Please, please turn me around and do what it takes so that when I come home, I won't be ashamed. I ask in Jesus' name for all these things. What do You want me to know today, Father?

**Day 102**

Father God,

Kathryn Kuhlman said, "To do God's will, we must come to the place where we have no will of our own." She went on to say, "When we want his will more than our own, and we know His will, we still have to submit to His will, even if we know it."

Somehow, I know she is right. I have set my will to do Your will, but I have never surrendered my will. To do Your will, I must give up my will entirely, not just tie it to Yours. When I tie it to Yours, it makes for a three-legged race—funny, but not very effective. I must give You my will.

To do that I must surrender my "I wants/needs/should/wills". These are all symptoms of self-management. To do Your will, I must let You manage my life, minute-by-minute and hour-by-hour. I must ditch my plans, my goals, my desires and simply say, "What do I do next?" every hour.

My own will is my enemy. It is in the way. It is a chain to me, a box that keeps me from fulfilling Your purpose.

I am only human and can't offer much, but I can be a living sacrifice. In Jesus' name, take my will? Help me, Lord God? What do You want me to know today, Father?

**Day 103**

Father God,

Glorious leader and abundant provider, I love Your provision! My portion is plenty in the midst of great poverty. Thank You for Your abundant blessing1

I need nothing for I am Your child. Income is irrelevant when I trust in You. What an amazing Father You are! Somewhere people are complaining about caviar and imported foods and I have the blessing of barbecued chicken. They are so poor! It is riches indeed to enjoy Your perfect provision. I have no desire to go where You are not appreciated. Your table is plenteous and full of meat and good foods.

Many look on my life with great pity and scorn. They have no clue that I am far more blessed just because I know You!

My apparent poverty causes me no separation from You! My lack of wardrobe does not shame me. Rather I appreciate You all the more for sparing me laundry, which I dislike to do! You are so wise! You give me just enough of what I need so I'm not distracted or trapped by it. You spare me the burden of a social life. You release me from the load of social approval. Pride does not cause me to stumble. Thank You for taking all of it! I love You for it! What do You want me to know today, Father?

**Day 104**

Father God,

Wonderful Father, as I wrote that I thought of a little child coming to kiss mommy or daddy so they can ask for candy. I can see them saying, "Oh, please?" and leaning over the arm of the chair for a hug. The child comes knowing that maybe daddy will say "yes", and maybe mommy "no"—but they ask anyway. Experience has proven that one of them will sneak them a piece of candy! Our children know us so well!

In just the same way, I feel Your love. I know that You would give us everything we ask for—if it were for our own good. You have to be the one who knows best in spite of being daddy who wants to bless. How hard it must be for You sometimes to say "no" when Your heart wants to say, "Oh, let them have it".

Thank You for being a good daddy. Thank You for not letting us have what would destroy us or disrupt our relationship with You! Owner of everything, You could give us everything we could imagine, but if You did we would no longer need You. How much better it is to need You! You are so much sweeter than possessions. All over the world people are losing all their possessions, but I can never lose You. Nothing can separate me from Your love. You are mine forever! Thank You! What do You want me to know today, Father?

**Day 105**

Father God,

It was so good of You to surprise me today. Thank You for good news and true blessings.

I appreciate Your handiwork more every day of my life! You are so good to me! No one takes care of us like You do! No one meets our needs like You do! Precious Father, thank You for taking care of Your own. It's good to be Your kid.

I wish everyone could know You like I do. I know that sounds superior, but every day with You is sweeter than the day before! I'm falling more and more in love with You as time goes by. Why don't people see that You love them and want to help them? Can't they feel how much You love them? If they could all experience this, they would never leave You. I know that only a few will find their way to everlasting joy, but oh, how I wish they all could. It makes me want to say, "Try harder." and "Seek longer.", and "Spend more time in the word". Our self-focused lives are such an obstacle to us. What a shame that we get in our own way so much. You are so faithful to those who do Your will. Thank You for being a good and trustworthy father. What do You want me to know today, Father?

**Day 106**

Father God,

Thank You for letting me dream! I love to think of what might be. And it is so good to know that everything I can dream about heaven will be twice as good! Your promises to us are guaranteed! All around us people fail us, but You never will! It is the continuity of Your love that is beyond humanity. We love and leave or lose and forget, but You will always love us—no matter what we do. Just as the father never stopped loving his prodigal son, You never stop loving Your prodigals. Just as I found joy when my prodigal son returned, I know it was so much more joy for You.

Daily You welcome us back to Your heart. Thank You! To know that we can never go far enough to be out of Your reach and covering is a comfort. Please forgive me for the years when I wandered away? I was so Young and hurt. I didn't know that by forsaking You I'd be hurt so much more. All the things that happened during those years have left me scarred, but the healing You have provided has been sweet and complete. I'm so glad You took me back and poured in the oil and the wine of Your Holy Spirit. Thank You for Your generous forgiveness! What do You want me to know today, Father?

**Day 107**

Father God,

I have so many questions to ask You. I could ask them here but I'd run out of paper. The good news is that I know that You have the answers and sooner or later I will know. Thank You for the answers You have already given me! Thank You for the knowledge that You let us have! It is amazing to me that You created us with the ability to learn. You have made us so complex. You threw in cell regeneration, self-healing by immune system, the ability to function without some parts and continuous growth to parts with hard usage, like nails. You even threw in adrenaline to get us moving when we should have been gone. You tossed in maturation hormones so we wouldn't have to be adults too soon! You added growth plates so our bones could keep growing. And You gave us an intake processor in our brain so we could learn from others and our own mistakes. You gave us a soft outer shell on a sturdy frame and hard shell for our fragile brain. And You designed our hands and arms for extreme flexibility!

Thank You for being so thoughtful! I love being an upright biped! What do You want me to know today, Father?

**Day 108**

Father God,

Your ways are unique! No one does what You do the way You do it. No one prepares the field for battle and wins the victory like You do. No one corrects our course and resets our direction like You do.

You are the map maker, the planet breaker, the mountain mover and the hope of all nations. We can't trust in anything but You!

You alone can build the heart. You construct the body of Christ one cell at a time. You apply the glue that holds it all together. You cover us like well-fitting skin. You protect us.

Thank You for Your words that bring us so much life! Thank You for Your promises that bring us hope for our future.

Blessed advisor! Beautiful God! No one compares to Your majesty! No one is even in the same category as You! You are unique! You are outside our realm of design and outside of our functional reality.

Holy, holy, holy God, Lord of Heaven and Earth, we bow to Your majesty. I surrender to Your call and purpose, Lord God. I surrender to Your work. Use my life as You see fit. I can bear any consequences, if You are with me as You always are. Hallelujah! What do You want me to know today, Father?

**Day 109**

Father God,

Tomorrow is a new day. Tomorrow Your will must be done just as it must be done everyday. It is great joy to know that obeying Your will always brings growth! To do what You desire is to walk a well-lit path on smooth round. No one can choose his or her own path and not walk on stony ground. To choose to walk on my own path is to choose to play hopscotch in a mine field.

Please forgive me for every time I disobeyed Your direct orders? I have foolishly chosen my own way many times. I have been blown up by my own will.

My desire is to serve You, but I am so easily distracted. My eye catches a movement and my head turns and I walk right on a land mine, hurt again by the enemy.

Help me to keep my eyes on Jesus? He is my light. He is my hope. Help me to know instantly when it is a distraction of the enemy and I should quickly look away? Help me to not get caught up in things that are not my business?

I ask these things in Jesus' name. Help me live so You are glorified? What do You want me to know today, Father?

**Day 110**

Father God,

Thank You! You are my faithful provider. Thank You for taking care of me! And most of all, thank You for assuring me that You are taking care of me.

I am dependent on Your mercy. The longer I know You, the more I know that I am dependent on You. Thank You for letting me know that I am safe with You! I can count on Your provision as long as I obey Your direction.

Thank You for making Your direction clear!

Thank You for the peace that comes with letting You do the work!

Wonderful, powerful God! Your ability to manage, direct, correlate, and choreograph our lives is amazing. You collate our lives as easily as stacking paper! The end result is a staggering composite of multi-faceted moving and functional being. It is glorious to behold Your handiwork.

You alone could pull off such a task. You alone are capable of even conceiving the idea. Our closest analogy is the human body with all of its complexity, but we are the first few lines of an artist's sketch compared to the grandeur You have created.

Your multi-level, fully-moving, alternating-speeds creation is astounding! And to be where I am and begin to comprehend it is far out! Way-to-go, God! What do You want me to know today, Father?

**Day 111**

Father God,

You are so cool! You plan is so over-reaching and all inclusive. Nothing is left out of Your plan.

I think of the fact that without evaporation we couldn't have rain and houses couldn't be dry. Dishes wouldn't dry and no one could be refreshed by a clear blue sky. Nothing is overlooked or out of Your control.

No one can fail to see the work that had to have been done by Your divine design! Just the fact that we can get water from the sky is amazing! All green growing things come from brown dirt! Most trees take a nap every winter and turn green again for spring. Flowers bloom every summer, whether they are tended by humans, or not. Regeneration is woven into Your plan as a source of joy, food and reassurance of continuation. You were obviously before the beginning and You alone can end the cycles.

We seldom recognize Your hand in our surroundings, the proof is everywhere. Forgive us our foolish vanity in taking credit for Your work? Without Your permission and guidance we could not build or assemble anything we consider "our" creations. Thank You for working through us! What do You want me to know today, Father?

**Day 112**

Father God,

Thank You for variety! We have so many choices! We are so spoiled in America! We can have so many things that we forget the people who live with no choices. We forget to be grateful for the choices.

Already I've forgotten the years when my choices were few. I complain because there is so many to pick from sometimes. Please forgive my foolishness? Please give me a grateful heart?

And Father, I ask You in Jesus' name to grant the requests of the very poor. Please give them jobs, clothing, food, and medical and dental help? Please provide education and job training for them and their children? And most of all, give them a hungry heart for You?

To find You I had to need You. Let them need You just enough, please? Give them peace that You are in control and will not let anything happen that is not for their overall good?

Let them have a taste of Your goodness so they will want more? Let them see a glimpse of what You have planned for them? Let them see that their poverty is a temporary affliction that is teaching them compassion, mercy and the dangers of judgment?

I ask so much, Father, because You are the holder of all things. I love You, and I know You love them. What do You want me to know today, Father?

**Day 113**

Father God,

Somebody is in dire straits right now. Please help them and let them know You are helping and have it all under control? Please show them that there is no loss that is accidental or unnecessary. All things are working together for the good of those You have called.

It comforts me so much, even as my life stays interesting, to know that You have it all under control! Your plan unfolds around me in tiny little pieces. Even as a puzzle may take thousands of pieces to assemble and no one sees the beauty of it until it is done, we see sections and connections come together to give glimpses of the whole.

You are the framer of our lives. You paint the primer, the background and the scenes. You choose the colors and those we will interact with. Like a flannel graph character we move around on our scene as we act and react to life. How much easier our lives would be if we would surrender our will and say, "You place me in the scene You choose, Father." We could save ourselves so much heartache if we would only stop and let You do it. Stick me where You want me, please. Forgive us our foolishness, Father? I ask in Jesus' name.

**Day 114**

Father God,

We are so foolish! We want the flowers but we get so involved with the weeds! We let ourselves get entangled in the things that don't matter so easily! We seek out tiny problems to fuss and moan about when we should just step back and thank You for wildflowers!

It's a focus thing, I think. I complain about my husband's dirty van instead of thanking You for the fact that I have my own and don't have to ride in his very often. I am so stupid! People all over the world would love to have a vehicle, much less two of them! And we have three! There's no reverse in the third one but it is a backup car. We are rich and complain about our blessings. So what if they are all 10 or more years old. We can go. I have forgotten about all the years I walked everywhere.

Father, please change my heart? Help me be an appreciative person instead of a whiner? Help me see my full cupboard and not say, "There's nothing I want to eat?" Help me thank You for so many clothes and not say, "I'm so tired of these?" Remind me often of the eight years with only two outfits.

Help me be the person You want me to be and the person others want to be around? I ask in Jesus' name. What do You want me to know today, Father?

**Day 115**

Father God,

We do so many things that are not in Your job description for our position. We take on so many things that are not our business. We take on projects You did not initiate. Why do we think that just because it looks good, we should do it? Why do we think that something should be done about something so we step up? It is arrogance.

You did not put me in charge of anything. You are in charge. You will fix it. You will straighten it out. You will reorganize it. You will get it done.

Remind me that when You gave us free will, You gave us the room to wreck our lives. But it's Your room! You know that whatever hurts us teaches us. Every time I wreck, I feel Your love. It teaches me to trust You! It teaches me to let You be the engineer and go sit in the passenger car and let You operate. You are so good at directing traffic and we, in our arrogance, think we need to help You.

Forgive me for my arrogance, Father?

Please help me let You be the pilot, engineer, driver, and church keeper? Guide me gently to my seat and show me the button for "Next assignment, please?"? I need to do only Your will—Your way. Please help me get me out of the way? In Jesus' name, I ask.

**Day 116**

Father God,

We occupy. We believe we own. We think we have property.

Scripture is clear. "The earth is the Lord's and the fullness thereof." I. Cor. 10:26 We are on borrowed land. We are temporary holders of temporary dwellings. As Solomon said in Ecclesiastes 2:21, "…it is vanity (all land passes to the next person)." How foolish we are to believe that flesh and blood has anything. Thousands of years of this planet have come and gone and we think we make a difference in our 100 years.

I bow to Your power. I surrender to Your purpose. Only as a functioning cog in Your machine can I make a difference. As part of Your team, Your plan can be fulfilled.

Father, please help us to see the futility of our own plans? Help us to be a part of the machine? Help us to recognize when I'm getting in Your way with my good ideas? Help me be part of Your operation? Better, help me to pray for its fulfillment and get out of the way of those who are better workers?

I need You, Father. I want to do for You—help me to not get in the way? Help me to trust Your leaders? I ask so much, forgive me, please? I ask in Jesus' name. What do You want me to know today, Father?

**Day 117**

Father God,

I am desolate today. I walk in a wilderness of pain. I am attacked without provocation and punished without cause. How long must I be punished? How long must I pay a price for a sin I did not commit?

The truth will exonerate me. When will they see the truth? When will my heart be seen?

No one knows the suffering they cause me. No one knows the hurt I have been through. How long must I endure this chastisement? I'm shouting into the desert for no one hears. No one understands.

How I wish I had Your perspective! I could see the whole forest then. I am surrounded by thorns and thistles, please cut me free?

Forgive me for my transgressions, Father? Forgive me my words spoken in haste and foolishness? A moment has been remembered forever; help me to be seen for what You have made of me? Help them to see the work You have done in me.

Great is Your faithfulness, Lord, great is Your love. I have learned so much. May I have a new lesson, please? May I begin again? May I see my salvation? I ask in Jesus' name and call upon Your mercy. What do You want me to know today, Father?

**Day 118**

Father God,

It is good to know that in Your eyes my sins are forgotten. Jesus paid the price for me and set me free from the wages of sin. The chastisement necessary for my peace was taken by him. His stripes paid for my healing.

Thank You for the peace, healing and forgiveness I feel. Thank You for the mercy that is new every morning.

The only new "thing" is mercy. Every day You give fresh mercy. Solomon said there is nothing new under the sun. He may have been right about natural things, but You are supernatural! You alone have the ability to do "new". And we know that You do new mercies every day! What a loving, incredible gift to us! Wonderful, Father!

It makes me think. If "mercy" is the only new thing, it must be at the top of Your list of important things.

What's on Your top ten list of "important"" items? What do You value most? Holy Spirit is our helper and the fruit of his help is given, "love, joy, peace, longsuffering, gentleness, goodness, faith, meekness and temperance". These nine and mercy makes ten.

What an elevated list to attain to! Please help all of us to become merciful, loving, joyful, peaceful, longsuffering, gentle, good, faithful, meek, and self-controlled, in Jesus' name? What do You want me to know today, Father?

**Day 119**

Father God,

All things are possible with You! Thank You! There is no mountain You can't move! There is no river You can't reroute. And there is no manmade obstacle that You can't surmount.

You are the author of our future and the recorder of our past. In Your book we are sin-freed and glory-destined. You note our kindnesses and acts of love. You record our goodness and works of righteousness. Thank You for letting me call on You as a friend. Thank You for letting me speak my heart, knowing that I won't be judged.

You have been rejected by Your own creation; You have felt the shame of exposure; You have been denied the honor You deserved. You understand my dilemma and don't judge me erroneously. Great is Your heart to me! Wonderful is Your love to me. You are my haven and my hiding place!

Although the storms of life attack from every side, You are there and under Your wings I can safely trust.

My foes shall not prevail!

My eternity is secure! My hope is in You, Lord, and it shall not be disappointed. You will be my rescuer. You are my salvation! What do You want me to know today, Father?

**Day 120**

Father God,

You are the giver of all healing. Why is it that we hurt the ones who can help us the most? We seem to inflict our meanest strikes on the ones who have done us the most good. Someone once said that "Christians are the only ones who shoot their own wounded".

I believe it is because Satan is out to destroy us, and, when we are down, he uses our loved ones to get in more kicks.

How cruel it is to judge one another! How foolish it is to say someone should or should not have done something. We do not know what led to any event. We do not know why anyone is motivated or deceived into doing anything. Forgive us, please? Our mission is not to judge but to forgive! Jesus said in Luke 23:34 "Then said Jesus, "Father, forgive them; for they know not what they do." As Stephen said in Acts 7:60, "Lord, lay not this sin to their charge."

We must all fight the flesh. We must all overcome the wounds of our past. We must all forgive those who wounded us.

I choose to forgive, Father. I have known pain. I ask You to forgive their sin against me and heal them.

Father, in Jesus' name, I ask You to save and deliver my enemies. What do You want me to know today, Father?

**Day 121**

Father God,

You are so wise. You give us our boundaries. You surround us with the things we need and people who will bring us life. You are in all ways and at all times right. Your ways are righteous altogether. Your promises are true and You always keep them.

Thank You for Your grace, giving me what I don't deserve. Thank You for Your mercy for not giving me what I do deserve!

Day in and day out I fail You. In all things I'm a stumbling fool and a bumbling idiot. Only with Your power and love am I able to face another day.

My enemies rejoice in my failures. My friends mock my attempts. I am rejected by those I love most.

You are my only comfort. You are my only consolation. In Your arms I am comforted by Your heartbeat. It is my assurance that all will be fine someday. All will be corrected and set right.

Forgive me, O God, for giving opportunity to the enemy? Forgive me for allowing myself to be careless?

Help me, Father, to be as wise as a serpent and as harmless as a dove? I ask in Jesus name. What do You want me to know today, Father?

**Day 122**

Father God,

Thank You so much for reassuring me. You always bring me peace. You are so good.

Benevolent and bountiful, You always meet our needs. It is good to know that everything everywhere is owned by You. You control who gets what and when they get it. I don't like to wait but I know that if You gave me everything I wanted when I wanted it, I wouldn't handle it right. You are so wise to ration out our blessings!

It is good to know how blessed we are. Thank You for letting me see how much better my life is than others. And thank You for teaching me not to even compare myself. Regardless of what I see, I now know that all of us have our own problems. It is wrong to decide someone has more or less than we have. Each of us has the portion assigned to us by You and is designed to help us. You know the plans You have for each of us. You know what it will take to get each of us to the place where we need to be.

Help me remember that every issue I face and every challenge of my life is designed to help me?

Thank You! You are so good!! Your ways are beyond comprehension, but Your love is evident. What do You want me to know today, Father?

**Day 122**

Father God,

Thank You for challenging friends!

Every time a friend does something so bizarre I wonder what planet they came from I have to thank You that I am more nearly normal. And even as I write that, I realize that normal is a book definition written by idealistic philosophers. For me, normal is not what I want to be!

Father, I ask You in Jesus' name to make me what <u>You</u> need me to be? Help me to set aside normal and acceptable and appropriate behavior? Help me to adopt the "norms" promised by scripture? Help me grow to the point where healing the sick is common as I pray for them? Help me to make myself available for Your work? Help me to care more what You think than what people think? Help me to bow to divine assignments and discard public approval?

We humans are all so caught up in "don't rock the boat" and "don't make waves" that we fight putting the boat in the water.

If that's what it takes, Father, throw me in the water! Shove me off the gangplank! Tell me to swim or drown!

It is far more important that I drown trying than that I never get wet! What do You want me to know today, Father?

**Day 124**

Father God,

Thank You for another proof today of Your work in my life. You alone could have brought circumstances and people together in such a way to cause such an event! Glory to Your name! You did it! You did it again! So many times in my life I have seen events come together spectacularly to Your glory! Thank You for one more example of Your sovereignty! You are sovereign in every situation, every life and every church. You are the only one who sees the whole picture and You always act for the person's eternal good!

It is assuring to see You do things so magnificently and to see You use humans with and without their knowledge.

We sometimes strut and claim to do things vaingloriously. How foolish of us to think "we" did anything! How grateful I am that You are in full control!

You are my righteousness! You are my holiness. You are master of the universe and You bless all of creation!

Mighty in power, gloriously splendid and majestic in honor, Father, I love You! What do You want me to know today, Father?

**Day 125**

Father God,

Thank You for victory in the midst of the battle! Thank You for help in the crises of our lives! You truly do hold our hands even when we appear to be surrounded by death and destruction.

All around me people are full of fears every day. Why can't they see that nothing matters? Truly nothing matters but what we do for You. We get all bent out of shape over events that won't matter a year or even a month from now. We fear events that are speed bumps to our destiny. We get caught up in issues that are of little significance to our eternity.

As I was told this morning, life is not about what happens. Life is about what we learn from what happens and what we do with that knowledge.

I ask You in Jesus' name to help me learn quickly and to do only what will glorify Your name, be in Your will or prepare me better for eternity? Help me to live full of faith and free of fear?

Help me work within You plan to fulfill Your purpose in my life? Help me to set my "self" aside and live totally surrendered to You? What do You want me to know today, Father?

**Day 126**

Father God,

One little, two little, three little praises; four little, five little, six little praises, seven little, eight little, nine little praises, ten little praises to You!

| | |
|---|---|
| Glorious! | Benevolent! |
| Wonderful! | Bountiful! |
| Mighty! | Beautiful! |
| Magnificent! | Righteous! |
| Holy! | Sovereign! |

Holy, Father God, You're my all in all!

Forgive me my silliness, Father, please? I am so full of joy today! Thank You for showing up at our meeting and cleansing us! Thank You for honoring our prayer with Your presence! Thank You for blessing us with Your work in our lives!

You are the best father ever! You acted to help us just when we needed You the most! As usual, Your timing was impeccable!

My joy is unspeakable!

Your goodness is unmatchable!

Your heart is too good to be described! What do You want me to know today, Father?

**Day 127**

Father God,

Thank You for categories! I like the new category. When "whatever" falls into "things that don't bring me life", it is easy to turn loose of them. I find myself turning off the TV when the show doesn't bring life.

Another category I like is "things I don't need". This one saves me money, especially when need is defined as "essential to life".

Another category—"no spiritual reason to go there or see that"—saves a lot of money.

All these categories are new to my life but I like them.

"Things not worth worrying about" includes everything, so I like it a lot.

"Things that are not my business" is a great category, too. "Saying only things that bless" is a category I'm trying to learn and I like the positive side of it. When temptation shows up, I like the category of "things to run from".

"Things to thank God for" is a big category that includes all the categories. Giggle!

Thank You for categories! Thank You for "things that give warning" like clues, symptoms, hints, visions, dreams and sirens. You are so faithful and protective. Thank You for minds that think of things to think about!

You are so generous to give us this built in self-defense system. What do You want me to know today, Father?

**Day 128**

Father God,

Thank You for knowledge! I just looked up "couth". It means, "marked by a high degree of sophistication, refined". I had thought I'd made it up, because I knew that uncouth was used to describe someone who was crude. Before You began working on me, I was uncouth and used to say I had no "couth"—thinking I was making up a word! I was right about not having couth, though. I wanted so much to be sophisticated and refined then. I still do.

Please forgive me? It seems so silly now to have wanted refinement for appearance sake. It was pride and ego talking. There are so many better qualities to desire!

It's been 41 years since You started open work on me; now I know that I need, and I ask in Jesus' name, for more love, compassion, and desire to help others. Will You please give me more energy, mental ability and money to help others with? Will You please give me discernment, wisdom and understanding? Will You please give me the right prayer for each situation I encounter?

Thank You for taking off many of my rough edges! Please "refine" me for Your use? Perfect me as a servant who will bring glory to You and make me a *spiritually* refined person? What do You want me to know today, Father?

**Day 129**

Father God,

Thank You for bringing me through the storm. I can hear the thunder in the distance and will always remember the horrible hail. The destruction was nearly complete but I have survived the heavenly stoning and now I must go on.

My heart was gravely wounded and I was left for dead, but that was not Your purpose.

I have forgiven all and will continue to pray for and bless my enemies. You allowed them to triumph for a season but You have defeated them.

My heart is clear. I will remember the lesson but I will not let my past consume my future with bitterness and gall. I will not live shy because I was burned.

Your gift to me was life and Your lessons are necessary. Thank You for the rod that built my character but spared my life.

It's time to move on now, Father. Show me the path I must take to fulfill Your purpose? Show me the next step?

Even as I have been cleansed and purified, fill me now with the joy of knowing that I am a good and trustworthy servant? Make me a Joseph?

I ask all these things in Jesus' name. What do You want me to know today, Father?

**Day 130**

Father God,

No one knows us like You do! Thank You for leading us into new directions! We can trust You when all around us is sinking sand. Our existence is a medley of traps and quicksand. Thank You for being the rock of my existence!

It is so disheartening to know that there are reefs along the shore. To know that there are dangers and traps on the way back to safety. Please keep me near the shore? Help me recognize Your path and not be led astray.

Many wise men and women have been led astray by the workings of their own mind. Many are the plans of a man's mind, but it is Your purpose that will stand, as scripture tells us in Proverbs 19:21.

Please guard my dreams and protect me from foolish endeavors? I am so prone to reach for rings that aren't there. I tend to reach for the ring and deny the jobs before me. Please, I ask in Jesus' name, keep me tied to the anchor? You and Jesus are my only hope.

Thank You for setting me up with Your plan for my redemption. Thank You for choosing me! Thank You for allowing Jesus to do what He did. What do You want me to know today, Father?

**Day 131**

Father God,

Thank You for letting us give! It is such a blessing to give, especially to kids! I love to see their faces when they open a present or a Christmas stocking. It is good to see them in my mind as they discover treasures. It gives me such joy to think about the things to put in and then to see You send in all the stuff! What fun it is to see You do such great things! And to know that You will use my little offering to touch a child's heart.

Thank You for showing me the joy of giving! I appreciate Your gift of joy so much! What an awesome God You are to let us know joy. We could make it our whole life without joy, but You gave me joy! Thank You!

I love to see You touch people and bring them to You. The multitudes of ways You use astound me!

Just the ways You use to draw us to Your heart are amazing! Every one of us was touched in some way individually and perfectly for us.

Wow! You are so cool! Thank You for letting us share in the wonder of Your love.

Amazing love! Amazing grace! Amazing blessings You give! Hallelujah! What do You want me to know today, Father?

**Day 132**

Father God,

Help me to live to be a blessing to others? Please help me put them first? I was born so selfish and self-centered, please help me be as Jesus said, "Be ye holy as I am holy." To be holy is to "live devoted to God and the things of God", according to my dictionary. Please help me stay devoted to You and Your things?

I get so caught up in my ideas and projects and dreams; please help me to work for You? Help me see when people are hurting? Help me know when to volunteer and when to stay out of the way?

So many times I've been a "busy Martha" instead of a "hearing Mary". Help me to hear first and work second? Help me know when a project is of You and when it is a dead work? To me a dead work is done in my own strength and my own wisdom and plan and is not Your idea at all. Good works done wrong are not good works at all. Help me remember that, please, Father? And help me do Your will right?

I believe Your blessing is on doing Your will, Your way, so please, in Jesus' name, help me obey? What do You want me to know today, Father?

**Day 133**

Father God,

Wonderful, wonderful, wonderful! You are multiple-times wonderful!

To know You is a thrill of joy and a delight to my very innermost being! You rock my world!

Nobody knows and loves You like I know we should! For all the good You do for us, we should show our love by making ourselves living sacrifices. That would truly be a reasonable service. But the more I know You, the more I know we should do so much more, because You are *sooo* good!

You are so generous with Your love. Thank You for pouring out Your love and grace and mercy to me!

You make me want to shout and dance and holler for joy, knowing how much You have done for me!

What joy to know that our eternal home will be even better! How neat to know that we will be surrounded by Your love when our time on Earth is over! We know Your love now, but we are so caught up in stuff now, then we can meet face to face!

Thank You for hope and a promise of even better things to come!

You are our dwelling place! What do You want me to know today, Father?

**Day 134**

Father God,

I don't know how to love. I can't seem to love like You do. Please help me?

So many times, I do something that hurts someone and then I realize it. I don't mean to do it; it just happens that way. Please help me realize it before I do it?

I read what love is in I Corinthians 13 and then think I have it, but the next minute or two find out I didn't.

Will You give me Your love for people?

People judge me and I get so mad I judge them back. Forgive me? Teach me how to pray? Tell me what to pray to shake this pattern?

Help me love as You do, without judgment or comparison or conditions? Help me be Your love to a hurting world? Help me be a true voice for You?

And please help me remember to put that cat out before I go to bed? I ask all this in Jesus' name.

And even as I read this aloud the cat came and insisted on loving me! Thank You, God! What do You want me to know today, Father?

**Day 135**

Father God,

Every day and in every way, Your ways amaze me! Your originality and creativity are superb! Your ability, agility and facility are sublime!

You think and it is done the moment it is spoken. Okay, I'm envious. I hate the drudgery of daily life. I hate to do anything I've done before, especially a few hundred times before. Which makes me think You should be sick at heart having to answer our simple prayers—the same prayers—over and over again!

What amazing patience You have! You can do it all and yet You answer "our" call! What a bunch of whiners we must sound like! But I know that even as we love our children, so You love us. You train us, just as we train our children. When we reach the point that we refuse to listen to their gripes anymore, we should remember that You don't need to hear us either. You know our situation better than we do. Just as we tell our kids—sometimes I have to work it out, walk it out and figure it out myself. Helping me isn't helping me if it prevents me from learning.

Help me remember to get myself back up, just as I made my children, Father? I ask in Jesus' name. What do You want me to know today, Father?

**Day 136**

Father God,

You rule in majesty. You are arrayed in splendor! Your throne is exalted in the heavens! You are higher, better, and wiser than all things!

You compose imagination and exceed limitations. You are the boundary maker. In light of Your glory, our attempts to achieve are feeble and foolish. You place authority in position and ordain ministry. No one is self-actualized. No one is self-made. We are purposeless outside of Your mercy and will. We are tools in Your hand.

But we are neither, if we "will" not to be. How foolish we are to fight Your purpose. In Your will is ease of mind. In Your will is satisfaction. In Your will is relaxation. In Your will is great peace.

Help me, Oh, God, to recognize when my "want to" gets in the way of doing Your will? Help me realize when my inborn rebellion rears its ugly head against Your purpose?

To step out of Your will is to step off a cliff. How dare I complain about the sudden stops. I should rejoice that You kept me from wandering further.

Help me remember that You are doing what I most need to prepare for all that You have planned for me? I ask in Jesus' name. What do You want me to know today, Father?

**Day 137**

Father God,

I love it when I see proof that You are answering my prayers! It is so evident that You are working on my children. Thank You! They are so convinced that they are adults that they won't listen to me. I know all kids go through this phase, but it's hard to watch. Just when they are old enough to understand deep spiritual things, they stop listening—groan!

Oh, oh, revelation time...

Just when we get old enough to turn into spiritual meat eaters, we think we are mature and stop seeking! Thank You for showing me that! It explains why so many people get some truth, decide it's the only truth, and guard it for the rest of their lives.

Remember the lady worked for 20 years for $1.00 an hour? She told me she did it because she was afraid to turn loose of what she had, even though others made over $3.00 an hour for similar work? I told her, "There's more work out there!"

There's more of You, too, Father. It's so stupid to assume that "my doctrine" is the only doctrine. Help me to constantly seek Your word for more revelation? Help me to never attach myself to a belief system that doesn't acknowledge new revelations? Help me read Your word to see what it says rather than look for what I want it to say?

Help me hear You and not blindly accept what people say?! I ask in Jesus' name. What do You want me to know today, Father?

**Day 138**

Father God,

Thank You for the potential for more! You, the author of all stories and holder of all futures, created potential. Thank You for Christian TV! I was listening just now and this came through! It was perfect for me now!

It's the "I don't know prayer":

1. Father, open the doors that need to be open to me and close the doors that are wrong for me.

2. Father, don't give me anything I can't handle.

3. Help me to understand the seasons of my life.

4. Take the people out of my life I don't need and bring the people in my life I do need.

(Pray it because I don't know a John from a Judas.)

You always know what we need and when we need it. It is 2 a.m. and I'm up and turned on the TV while I snacked and wrote to You. I didn't expect You to speak to me. I'm so glad You don't wait until I expect You.

I'm so glad You don't limit how You speak to me. So many things are revealed in so many ways, it's good. How can people assume that You only speak in one way? You are the father of creativity! I never do any thing the same way twice. With Your infinite ability, why would anyone assume You use "one" way of doing anything? Help me to receive whatever You say, however You may say it? I ask in Jesus' name. What do You want me to know today, Father?

**Day 139**

Father God,

I enjoy music! I don't listen often and often what I get is not directly Christian but every song has a message. Some of the old songs come to mind now and each one has a story to it. Some have a sentiment, some have an encouragement, some have a message of hope, and others build me up. A few songs even worship You, Father. But I'm noticing that if I could sing all of the sings ever written, I will never fully express the love in my heart for all that You have done for me.

Remember when I used to try and write songs? Oh, how You must have groaned. In Your mercy, You didn't let me have a singing voice or an ear for music. Now I know that with my personality that would have been a disaster! My gifts are a perfect tool for me to fulfill Your plan for my life. My gifts enable me to learn what I need, to be what You need me to be. Please help me remember that a gift in the wrong hands is an ugly thing? I ask in Jesus' name. What do You want me to know today, Father?

**Day 140**

Father God,

Thank You for poverty! Thank You for limiting my buying power!

I get so distracted by "things" that it has been a blessing to not have them. It has simplified my life so much to not have too many clothes to pick from. And it has removed from me the façade of "gotta". When I didn't have, I didn't do the "gotta do" things the world demands and I'm fine. Poverty has shown me that the only "gotta" is that I must prepare for eternity—You will even take care of death and taxes!

You promised to meet my needs and You have done so in many ways, with and without money.

I'm convinced that poverty has helped me so much! I have learned that I can and will make it through anything. I have lost my pride. I have learned mercy as I suffered the unjust judgments of people because I couldn't do what they thought was a mandatory "gotta". I've learned not to impose standards on others. I've learned patience as I waited for everything. I've learned to give the best because people occasionally gave me their worst. I've seen You supply my needs in so many ways it blows the mind. And I've learned to appreciate You so much more than if I had "done it all by myself". You are so good to me and You are all that matters! What do You want me to know today, Father?

**Day 141**

Father God,

You are so wise.

I need Your wisdom. Thank You for sending it to me by so many means.

Even as my situation seems desolate and hopeless, You have encouraged me! Help me to encourage others? All of us have our desert times sometimes. Help me to make the most of my wilderness? Show me what I still need to learn here now so I won't have to come back later?

I know there are green pastures over the next hurdle, but please don't let me jump too soon? I've gotten so I can stand the desert now. I wouldn't want to have to acclimate again. I've had wonderful times with You in the solitude. And I've learned that even cactuses bloom. Thank You for showing me the blessing of anonymity and barrenness.

I've grown much hardier and more capable by using only what was given; help me to never again think that I must "have" to do? Help me remember that the product of "make do" materials often has much more character?

What else do I need to learn? I am waiting in the night for Your instruction. Help me, Father? I ask in Jesus' name. What do You want me to know today, Father?

**Day 142**

Father God,

Nobody does anything as awesomely as You do!

You order our footsteps and set us in the perfect situation for each of us. It is Your privilege to see the value of each of us and to place us where our individual gifts can be expressed. I like Your administration talent! You impress me with Your managerial abilities! You prioritize and synchronize all the details of our daily operations with ease.

Father, Your coordinate personnel, shipping and handling, and consumption with finesse! Your year end reports must be awesome. Your budgets are always balanced.

I'm impressed with Your absolute comprehension of all needs in all departments and especially Your coordination of our interactions.

Your business savvy on the enterprise of Earth is complex and extends beyond computer capability.

Father, You are the chief operating officer of all the chiefs and yet You are willing to talk to me! I'm so humbled to know that You will acknowledge me and that You love me. Thank You. What do You want me to know today, Father?

**Day 143**

Father God,

Thank You for being so thoughtful of us! You gave us pets! Thank You for pets!

I get so aggravated at that cat that wants out at 4:30 a.m., but I love to see that same cat warming up my chair in a comical position. I love to see her play!

That silly dog of ours chases in her sleep, goes night-seeing (sits out during the night), and is a one-man fan club for my husband. She adores him and makes up to him for all the other things he can't afford to have.

You even let us have a guinea pig who ate anything grown and lived twice as long as most piggies.

All of them have made us laugh and entertained us when we needed it most. All of them have provided conversation when the switch was needed to keep the peace. All of them have provided mini-fight material when we needed to vent but shouldn't vent on each other. And all of them have provided comfort when we needed someone or something with skin on.

Thank You for being so awesome! Thank You for being so incredibly considerate of our needs!

You are the best, the most, the ever-wonderful, sweetest father ever! What do You want me to know today, Father?

**Day 144**

Father God,

Thank You for my health! I am so grateful that I can still walk and talk and do the things I need to do. I am so happy to have a sharp mind and a ready pen. Thank You!

I know that You order my steps and I thank You for setting me up with a home and my own vehicle. Thank You for daily provision!

You are always and, in every way, deliberate. I used to be so angry at the events of my life, but now I see that they have shaped me and made me who I am today. You have established me. You have built and renewed me by regeneration of my mind. It must have hurt so bad when I wandered so far from You. I'm so glad to be back! I'm so glad to know that You took me back! Thank You for putting up with me.

Thank You for forgiving me of so many sins. You are holy, wholesome, righteous and good! You have done so much for me! You are far more generous with Your forgiveness than we have any right to expect! You are our only hope and our only destination. I seek You with all my heart and desire to see You daily. Thank You, Father, for all You are! What do You want me to know today, Father?

**Day 145**

Father God,

Almighty, omnipresent Father, where are You? I need You. I seek You! I want to spend my days in Your love and in the fullness of Your presence. Help me jump all hurdles in the path? Help me run the race to win? Help me buffet my body so I'll be in shape to be all that You need me to be?

I am abandoned without You. I am lost in a desolate land, without life and deserted. I am despondent in Your absence. Please, Father, come to me? I can't live here without You. I need Your love and Your presence. I need Your daily counsel and teaching.

Help me overcome all obstacles to You?

Break me, shake me, sift me and crush me. Remove all impurities and bleach all imperfections. Renew my mind and regenerate my spirit that I may maintain a clean connection to You. Please?

Help me, Father. I am bound by flesh and habits. I am cursed by humanity and transgressed by teachings. Help me set it all aside and see only You and Your will for me?

I ask in Jesus' name. What do You want me to know today, Father?

**Day 146**

Father God,

Thank You for using every available media to reach the world! I love to know that I can turn on TV at any hour and be blessed. I love to know that I live in a free country! I can speak, share and worship freely. Thank You!

I ask in Jesus' name, to bless those who are seeking You in countries that are not free. Help every person in every situation to find You! Help them! Reveal Yourself to them! Show Yourself faithful to them! Show Yourself! Let them know Your power! Let them experience Your presence! Release to them Your provision!

Father, let them know You as I know You—Awesome, Holy, Powerful, and Wonderful!

You are total, all-encompassing, pervasive, and fully-enabled to do any single complex glorious thing! Please show the world that You are their source! What do You want me to know today, Father?

**Day 147**

Father God,

Thank You for teaching me the therapeutic and relief value of prayer! I never would have thought that prayer for others would do so much for me!

When I was so miserable from coughing around the clock for two weeks with pneumonia, I prayed for others more miserable than me for the first time, remember? And immediately I was still sick but not miserable—and a week later I was completely well, without the aid of a doctor! Since then You have heard from me about others every time I felt bad or sick or miserable. And every time I felt better and knew someone else would be better, too!

Thank You! Thank You for bringing misery to me so I could learn this. Thank You for letting me experience some suffering that led to a greater good! Thank You for so much. You are so awesome! My discomfort was such a tiny thing compared to the good it brought. Now when others tell me they don't feel well, I always help them. I'm so glad You helped me feel their pain! What do You want me to know today, Father?

**Day 148**

Father God,

I love to pray for people who can't pray for themselves and I know You love that! Thank You for showing me this and helping me think of prisoners in other countries, little children, paralyzed and deformed people, abused and used people and the list goes on...

So many people have been silenced or haven't heard of Your love.

The deaf and dumb in so many countries and nursing home residents who can't care for themselves and are being neglected need Your help. The tiny child whose sick and perverted parents are hurting him or her needs Your help. Those who are very alone and old need Your help as well. Those trapped in prisons of their own mind need You, also, Father, please help them?

Please do what's best for every category I mentioned here? I ask in Jesus' name. What do You want me to know today, Father?

**Day 149**

Father God,

I pray for the person who may someday be reading this.

I ask You, Father, in Jesus' name to heal this reader's spirit, soul and body. I ask You to meet their needs spiritually, physically and mentally. I ask You to provide mental, spiritual and physical nourishment for them. I ask You to bless their families, work environment, homes, vehicles, neighborhood and fellowship groups. I ask You to bless their finances, teach them money management and give them a desire to give to Your work in every way, especially financially.

I ask You to create in my reader a clean heart, renew a right spirit and never take Your Holy Spirit from them.

I ask that You help them surrender themselves as willing sacrifices. I ask You to help them surrender their members (tongue, arms, legs, talents and minds) as instruments of righteousness.

Finally, I ask that You pour on him or her the gift of repentance that will enable confession and healing of every incident in his or her life. What do You want me to know today, Father?

**Day 150**

Father God,

Nobody knows You. We can't begin to describe Your composite of abilities. We can't begin to say what You can't do. I am ashamed of the times when I've said, "God doesn't do that". Please forgive me if I erred in saying that?

Please break down any walls I may have built that keep You from acting in me or through me? Help me stay in the word so I recognize when You are speaking? Help me do what You need me to do?

No one can ever limit You, but we limit what we receive from You. We cut off our own blessings because we won't accept a different way of something happening.

I repent of ever saying, "That's not the way God does things". Who am I to judge? Who am I to put You in a box? I'd be a fool to say You are unable to do anything! Forgive me, please, for deciding for You Your capabilities?

I ask in Jesus' name. What do You want me to know today, Father?

**Day 151**

Father God,

Thank You for new input from new sources! I love to learn something new that helps me grow spiritually. I love to find something in the news or on TV or the internet that reassures me that You love us. You are so cool to help us in so many ways!

Yours is the power and glory forever and ever! You are the creator of all new things! Shame on me for ever thinking that You were limited to "one" anything! You use such a variety of means to get through to us! You are so awesome!

You are the author of all media—although I'm embarrassed by much of the content. Thank You for letting the good come in as well.

Thank You for not fitting in my box! Thank You for not being limited to what this messed up human can conceive!

Holy, righteous, wonderful Father! You deserve all that we have and are! What do You want me to know today, Father?

**Day 152**

Father God,

Somebody is hurting today. Please help them and heal them? It's a pain that keeps coming and it has them worn out. Please heal the cause of the pain?

Someone somewhere is caught in a trap that is tormenting their soul and spirit. Please set them free?

A child somewhere is being abused out of the cruelty of a sibling. Please heal the child and stop the sibling?

Somewhere an older person is lying in pain and unable to get up. Please send them peace, help and comfort, and then heal them?

Somewhere there is someone caught between lies and accusations that aren't true. Please intervene for that person with a divine solution?

Somewhere someone is interfering with Your work in a life by "helping" when they shouldn't. Please prevent the "helper"?

I ask all this in Jesus' name. What do You want me to know today, Father?

**Day 153**

Father God,

Thank You for mothers. My mom would have been 85 now. It's hard to believe she's been gone for 42 years. She wouldn't know what to think of me now, sitting here writing letters to You! I miss her still sometimes, and I know my life would have been much different if she had been here.

I have been mentored by so many good women now. I'm so grateful that You filled the gap for me. I've been loved by wonderful people sent by You. I'm so glad You sent them.

Through all the good and bad people in my life You have been a steady source of love and encouragement. Thank You! I need people with skin on, but every day I need You more. I want to be with You so much. I love You so much. In all the years I've known You, You have never failed me. Thank You for being bigger than description! I love You! What do You want me to know today, Father?

**Day 154**

Father God,

My life stays so interesting. It seems there is always a change of some kind. It makes me wonder how much more I can take. Your word says You will never put on us more than we can bear, but just now I'm pretty bent.

I can do all things through Jesus who strengthens me, but I must be tapping him pretty dry at this point.

I've known since before I started school that my life would be a hard climb. I don't think I had any idea how hard. This uphill stuff feels like Mt. Rainier lately.

Is there a slide on the other side? Or maybe a nice parachute ride down would be nice. Do You have one of those rope slides waiting? A helicopter at the top so I could see the whole view would be great.

It's okay if there isn't. Someday I'll be with You all the time and it will all be worth it.

For now, could I walk the nearest ledge for a season? My muscles could use a break. I love You and I ask in Jesus' name. What do You want me to know today, Father?

**Day 155**

Father God,

I am heart-weary. I can't think of words to describe my situation. I find myself in quicksand in the middle of a ballroom. I feel as needed as more rain in a flood. I feel as welcome as in-laws moving in. The facts of my existence contradict my appearance.

My past, present and future are all in Your hands. Unless You intervene, my life is worthless. For the first time in my life, I begin to understand despair. I've seen desolation; but have never seen so little hope. I live a conflicted existence. I know that there is no way You will not fulfill Your purpose for me. I know that You will preserve me. But at this point in time, all I can see, feel and experience is a very tiny ship alone on a great big sea and sinking fast. In view of this, I need to ask in Jesus' name that, if You would, could You please do something to give me a little hope? What do You want me to know today, Father?

**Day 156**

Remember the door analogy of life where You have to choose the right doors? I could use a door. Any door would do at this point since the one I entered by seems to have disappeared.

My life is turning out to be a creative fiction work that most people don't comprehend, least of all me. I'm starting to feel like a game piece that gets moved but can't move on its own. I'm ready for a new square, by the way.

I've enjoyed being the game piece. It has relieved me from having to make decisions and make choices. I'm not good at choices. I pick what looks good and then find out it just looked good.

By nature, I'm a player who seems to have married the board. The choices we make are sometimes a little incredulous, aren't they? But I look back at how much I've learned form the board and it's been good.

Thank You for closed rooms and game boards! What do You want me to know today, Father?

**Day 157**

Father God,

I feel like I'm in prison but it is self-made. I have hamstrung myself. I have welded myself to an anchor then thrown myself overboard. But You are sovereign.

Never mind what I've done; You are able! You are capable. You can cut the weld. You can heal the hamstring. You can open the doors.

Hallelujah! Hallelujah! You rule! You reign! You are unstoppable. No matter what the circumstances, what I feel or see; Your word is working mightily in me! You will perfect me.

All I see is the box. You are the holder. You see it as an entryway. It's small to me; but turn me around and I'll see the door. Turn me, Father, please? I ask in Jesus' name. Turn me? What do You want me to know today, Father?

**Day 158**

Father God,

I need Your hand. Use it on my backside and get me adjusted, please? Fix my attitude manually; I can't seem to fix it myself. There is rebellion in me. I can't get going, please smack me one and get me started?

I'm like a car in the mud. My wheels are spinning but I am not getting anywhere. I'm not moving.

Give me a shove, please? Send me a tow truck and drag me out?

I can't wait for the sun to dry out the mud, but I'd be wasting work time. Please send me to a new job!

I'm ready to ditch this old truck and move on to a new location, a new vehicle and a new ministry. I'm sorry, I don't mean to tell You what to do. I am just wasting gas here and could use some new scenery. Please, in Jesus' name, do something about my situation. What do You want me to know today, Father?

**Day 159**

Father God,

Metaphorically speaking, I'm on a roll. I've got my motor started. I'm stumping. I'm on my soap box. I'm swimming with the stream. But it's all words that do not matter.

I am asking one more time for You to do that final bit of lipo-word and cut the dead weight off of me and let me run. I want so much to go for You! You are so good to put up with me! You are so wise to keep me on a short chain, but please, I want a new cage of some kind. Let's leave the old bones buried here and go find a new spot to dig. Maybe there's a well-needed spot ahead.

Paul said he was running the race. I want to run, too. I'm set in concrete here and I want out. I'm chomping at the bit. I want to show my stuff.

I must not be ready, so one more time I have to say, "Your will be done"!

Meanwhile, I do trust You and Your decisions! I will always love You. What do You want me to know today, Father?

**Day 160**

Father God,

Why do people do the stupid things? One more time someone is refusing to do the smart thing; because they don't "feel like it"; because they don't like the way it was presented. I see it so much. Mom used to say, "He's cutting off his own nose to spite his own face". He's refusing to do the right thing, because of the way he sees the situation. The person I'm thinking of has an imagined pain. His leg hurts, so he shoots himself in the foot so he won't have to walk it out. After awhile he'll be walking pretty crippled, I'm thinking. He is shackling himself in the middle of the race.

Metaphorically speaking, I'm a poor writer, but I'm trying to say that I see this person making a mess of their life over his human perception despite what others tell him is the right thing to do (and they're right)!

Have I ever done that? Of course, I have. Please show me the specific instances so I can repent of them? Please help me dig out my self-inflicted bullets? Help me cut my own shackles? And please do some heavenly plastic surgery on my face? My nose gets stuck up, too.

And Father, please give wisdom to me and him? You know who I'm talking about. Please show him the foolishness of his rebellion? Help us overcome ourselves? I ask in Jesus' name. What do You want me to know today, Father?

**Day 162**

Father God,

As usual, Your timing is perfect! It seems that I write so many exclamation points to You, but whatever You do is always in the "so" and "very" and "awesome" categories. It befuddles me that people can't see Your handwork in their lives and the lives of those they love. We are dense dummies, I'm afraid. It took me awhile to figure out that You are in control. Of course, I don't like the fact that people get hurt. But I know that eternity is a lot longer than life. You can hurt me all it takes here to make sure I'm good for eternity.

My life stays interesting, but I know that You have allowed it for an eternally good result.

Thank You for not making my life easy! I wouldn't have needed You and found You if I was comfortable! What do You want me to know today, Father?

**Day 163**

Father God,

How easily You change the directions of our lives. We have a full life and are set in it; and in an hour it is gone. An hour was all it took to destroy me.

I guess these are the trials of our lives. I've had more than a few, I think. I'm looking at my next occupation (maybe) and wondering why the last one had to go. But it's funny—I don't mind. I wouldn't have You this close to my heart if You hadn't shut me down. I knew the rock could fall; I just didn't expect a boulder! It was hard, but I like me now that I'm flattened.

The next question is—isn't it time to scrape me off the floor and move on? I'm getting a little too comfortable down here.

Whatever You want, I'll do it. At this point, I'm Your very willing but somewhat immovable pancake.

By the way, the sky is gorgeous. Thanks for slowing me down and laying me out so I could enjoy the heavens! What do You want me to know today, Father?

**Day 164**

Father God,

Thank You for the unexpected blessings. I love it when You surprise me with something. Maybe it was something I wanted to do or a movie I'd heard about. Maybe it's a phone call I didn't expect or a visitor. It seems to always come just when I need a pick-me-up.

By now You have picked me up so many times You must have spiritual backache.

Thank You for the lifts! By now I'd have road rash on my face if You had not helped so many times. Thank You! And thanks for the one time I really did have road rash on my face—what a nice lesson about being careful!

And those lifts were all blessings, too, now that I think about it. You could have left me down there. Now that I'm halfway back up, the view is so much better! So is the outlook. My Bible school teacher once said that when things look bad, look up—the up-look will improve the outlook. Thanks for the new outlook—only You can rearrange the view—and it is awesome! What do You want me to know today, Father?

**Day 165**

Father God,

Days, months, seasons, years all go slipping by these days. I remember when a year took forever. But now a year is a blink of an eye. How quickly Your thousand-year-days must go for You. I remember the lines,

"Only one life, 'twill soon be past;

Only what's done for Christ will last". From the poem by C.T. Studd of the same name.

It helps me remember that You have given us so few years to live and only what we do for You is of any value for eternity.

Why do we worry so much about today? Today is a blip on the screen. Life is about the whole screen and all the parts behind the screen. We can't see the whole "monitor" but we will someday. Please help me mind my own line and not worry about other people's blips? Help me not to get caught up in their errors and keep myself straight instead?

You are so faithful to help me. Please help me leave a good record? I ask all these things in Jesus' name. What do You want me to know today, Father?

**Day 166**

Father God,

I want to thank You for not answering all of my prayers. Some of them would have done me great harm if I had had them granted. And some of them would have hurt others as well. Some would have set me back instead of bringing me forward.

The longer I love You, the more I appreciate Your wisdom. You always do what is best for me in the eternal run and that proves how much You really do love me.

It's easy to give into a child's requests, but if You really love them You know that sometimes You have to say "No". Thank You for saying no to me when I would have made a grievous mistake. Thank You for not letting me have the things that would have kept me from You. Thank You for the eighteen years of chronic, acute, debilitating poverty. The things I did without don't mean anything now. The things I gave up that I didn't need have made me so much better! I sure didn't need that pride problem I had and, in many areas, it is gone now! Someday, maybe, it will all be gone. I have learned so much love, grace, and mercy through it all as well.

Thank You for being a great "Dad" to me. What do you want me to know today?

I love You! Me.

**Day 167**

Father God,

Sometimes I think You and Jesus must get so impatient with us. I'm thinking that it is hard for You not to tell Jesus to go on back to Earth. But I also know that Your love wants everyone to be saved. You don't want any to perish. I'm so eager to see the end times and I know they have already begun.

Thank You for telling us what types of things to expect! You are so good. You could have just said, "I'm coming, be ready". But You didn't. I'm glad we can read the times and see it coming quickly.

It is so close. Because it is, I ask You, in Jesus' name, to send forth harvesters to collect the lost. Impart to them the urgency of this situation. Impart to the lost their sinful and death-bringing condition. Grant to the workers of the harvest a supernatural wisdom and knowledge that will enable them to win as many as possible. What do You want me to know today, Father?

**Day 168**

Father God,

No disrespect intended, but what were You thinking when You invented the skunk? I like the porcupine idea. I even can understand the armadillo thing. But skunks get everything in range, not just their attacker—or whatever scared them. And right now, I can't imagine what my window air conditioner did. This house really stinks!

Come to think of it; it was stinky, musty, and bad before the skunk. We have become such hermits that the house needs fresh air! Today I was thinking about how we never needed fresh air when the kids were slamming doors in and out all day. I never saw the blessing of fresh air then.

How many times have You met our needs and we didn't know it—and certainly didn't thank You? I just never saw the daily provision of a dry roof and soft bed. I never think of refrigeration, running water and flush toilets. Thank You, Father! Thank You for all the things that You do that we never thank You for. What do You want me to know today, Father?

**Day 169**

Father God,

Solomon wrote that, "He who trusts in the Lord shall be made fat" (Proverbs 28:25b). From the looks in my mirror I seem to be really trusting! I'm laughing, but the truth is, I really do trust You after all these years.

Remember when I tried to help You fix things? You must have groaned, got mad, or laughed Your head off. I'm ashamed to say it now, but I honestly thought that from what I could see, (I knew what needed done.) that You needed my help. The problem is that I'm seeing from my perspective, which is so limited! You see and know from all perspectives. It is so much easier now to stop and let You deal with situations—and especially people.

I love it when You deal with people and get them to do things I can't! It is a hoot to pray that they will surrender to You and ask You to deal with them. Nobody can argue with You! Thank You for being such an awesome God! What do You want me to know today, Father?

**Day 170**

Father God,

I'm freaked out. I know that some really weird stuff went down in my work situation. At this point I'm being <u>told</u> by humans on all sides that I should get a job. But it seems that all I'm getting is closed doors. I've never had this situation before. After 53 jobs, I've just assumed job number 54 would come along. I've been hoping for my final job for the last decade or so but my life has never been so secured. It's been really good for me, because I am now completely secured to You. The questions are these, "What do <u>You</u> want me to do about work? Have I had my last job yet? Am I on Your payroll now?"

Hope deferred makes the heart sick (Proverbs 13:12) and I'm getting pretty sick lately. So…in Jesus' name, I ask You for a full confirmation of what I am to do, by any means You choose. Please? What do You want me to know today, Father?

**Day 171**

Father God,

Sitting here with believers in fellowship, I seem to have forsaken my own for the weirdest bunch of Christians ever. I've never met a normal Christian that wasn't abnormal to the world! As long as You're with me, I seem to be comfortable anywhere. You are my peer group. You are my comfort zone.

It doesn't matter if the car seems to be surrounded by lake or the ship is on main street—the reality is that nothing but eternity is reality!

The pleasure is mine to know that You are always near in the midst of whomever—especially since it doesn't matter where they are in my life.

In the crowd or alone on the road, You sustain me with sweet precious love. Your love is my lifeline; please don't ever take it from me? What do You want me to know today, Father?

**Day 172**

Father God,

Thank You for the answer to my prayer of forty years. It is amazing that Your timing is so perfect. In the hour of my greatest preparation You have added a valuable tool.

There is no one like You, Father.

There is no one else who could see the harm it would have done to have answered that prayer of forty years a day sooner. Truly Your decisions are divine.

By the granting of Your gift, I can fulfill Your purposes for my life well. Thank You! It is marvelous to me that You consider me able to receive such a wonderful gift. It amazes me that You have chosen to do anything for me and now You bless me so much!

You are wondrous in glory, beautiful in majesty, and divine in manifestation. Holy, holy, holy, Lord God Almighty, You have always been and always will be, the rewarder of the faithful!

Hallelujah! What do You want me to know today, Father?

**Day 173**

Father God,

I am so tired and so full of joy! I'm befuddled again! I love what You have done in my life this weekend! I adore the gift this whole weekend has been to me!

To know that You love me so much to do so much for me is incredible! Thank You!

Glorious, marvelous, wonderful Father, Your goodness and generosity are exceedingly beyond mere human capacity. You are love. Your love exceeds our ability to comprehend. I am just beginning to grasp the depth and breadth and height of it. I can see the shadows of the multiple dimensions of Your love in Your grace and mercy and patience with us.

We are woefully incapable of beginning to mimic what You are effortlessly. Please help me to love as You love? Help me to extend grace and mercy to all? I ask these in Jesus' name. What do You want me to know today, Father?

**Day 174**

Father God,

You alone can see the devastation in my heart. You can see how heartsick I am. You know that my sins are grievous and the punishment deserved. You know that my life is demolished. You are the only one who can use the pieces! You are the only one who can make beauty from the ashes.

Thank You for the hope for a future. Thank You for letting me know that at least You still love me. You know that I am judged by friends, foe and family. Please forgive me for judging others? Please cleanse my heart and soul? Please restore what the worm has eaten? I am consumed day and night. I am defeated and destroyed. All that is mine is Yours completely. All that is left is Yours. As the creator of dirt, I know that You alone can make me into usable elements. I offer You the dirt I am. In Jesus' name, I ask You to take me and do what is best for me? What do You want me to know today, Father?

**Day 175**

Father God,

Thank You for being so "right on". I know it isn't said any more but You are so "cool"! You are the "coolest dude" ever! "Righteous dude!"

Many times our slang has changed but Your description has always been done using the superlatives. You are the "most", the highest, the best of all!

You are always "on target". I'm "up" with You and I "dig You". "Awesome dude!" You are so "groovy"! You make "my heart sing"! You are the "beef"! "You go, God!"

Our descriptive vocabulary continues to evolve, but the last word is this: We will never be able to describe with any slang or vernacular language the full measure of how good, wonderful and comprehensive You are. No matter how much we know "You rock!", we will always be creations on the rock. As Your created beings, we can't describe our creator. But we love to try because You are so "neat"! What do You want me to know today, Father?

**Day 176**

Father God,

No one can come close to Your overall exceedingly, great, performance record! No one's work can compare to Your operational standard or execution of sequence. No one can come close to matching Your quality control or Your quantity maintenance. You have exceeded human ability for production quotas, standards and quality in every known category! You are the best of the best, unmatched, unrivaled and poorly imitated by the best of us.

No one can match Your ability to manage, balance and produce all things for our good and our edification. You are the CEO of CEOs!

You are the most organized and best choreographed of all! You create, distribute, and manage single-handedly with skill and finesse. You are my model of performance. What do You want me to know today, Father?

**Day 177**

Father God,

I admire Your patience with Your patients. As one of the walking wounded, I need Your healing touch and restoration. I need the balm of Gilead and the oil of gladness.

I need Your loving touch of comfort and peace. You are the sweetest of all caretakers! Your touch brings healing to our soul and spirit.

Father, I know that I have allowed poisons to enter my body in various forms. I've allowed evil to creep in attached to good. Will You remove it, please? Will You put me on the operating table and use Your scalpel and forceps and pull it back out? Will You incise the ruined sections and reattach the healthy tissue? Will You fix my damaged heart? Will You replace the bad values and strip the clotted arteries? Will You make me whole again so I may serve You with full and unhampered vitality? I ask these things in Jesus' name. What do You want me to know today, Father?

**Day 178**

Father God,

Finest of the fine and purest of the pure, You are beyond the beyond. You are the nicest of the nice. You are greater than the great. You exceed the excessive.

When I try to describe You, I'm stumped. There are no combinations of letters and words that will adequately convey even my minute comprehension of the extent of Your being. I can't add prefixes or suffixes that will increase the meaning to a depth that could begin to convey Your breadth of being. I can't build a sentence syntax that will carry the depth of meaning You possess. There is no paragraph structure that appropriately shapes a discussion of Your capacity.

All my attempts to compile a description are met with failure because You are bigger, wider, deeper, longer and more intense than our words can describe. Forgive me for putting forth my dismal attempts, please? What do You want me to know today, Father?

**Day 179**

Father God,

Why did You share with us the ability to get great ideas? I know we are made in Your image so You get them, too. But I get frustrated when I can't do mine. I hope You don't. And I hope, like me, that You don't do every idea. I'm sure it has occurred to You to wipe us out and start over—thanks for not doing that again. It may have occurred to You to see what we would look like with elephant ears—again, thanks for not doing that!

I'm glad You didn't decide to see how we would manage without fossil fuels or wheels. I'm also glad You didn't decide to remove all tools.

These are silly thoughts, I know, but they remind me that You are not capricious or careless, and You love us enough to do the best for us—no matter what it looks like to us.

And thank You for the idea for electricity! What do You want me to know today, Father?

**Day 180**

Father God,

I got my dates mixed up again just now. I get so many things mixed up. For years I thought my family was more important than You. I should have taken time for You; there was plenty of time for the family.

And as it turns out there will be more family! An unexpected blessing is on the way! I love these tiny treasures! I hope it is a big healthy baby. Of course, it won't be mine, it will be another borrowed treasure, but it will be loved. You chose to bless my nephew; I just hope he realizes this is a blessing.

I ask You in Jesus' name to protect this baby, provide for it, and keep it loved and welcomed its whole life. Let the mother be loved and appreciated as well, for as long as she lives. Let the baby be given great gifts and a great love for You? Bless it with patience and understanding from the start?

Let this baby the most loved, wanted and treasured baby I know, please? I ask in Jesus' name. What do You want me to know today, Father?

**Day 181**

Father God,

It has been an interesting day. I was able to give, love, and help someone. I wish everyday could be like that.

I'm frustrated now though. I could have done some real good if I could have prayed with the people. They needed *Your* help so much more than the practical things I could do.

You must want so much to help us. Knowing I could make things better if they would let me connect them to You is frustrating.

How can I do the things that really matter? How can I help them in eternal ways?

Father, what, if anything, have You been trying to tell *me* and help *me* with? What do *I* need to know that I haven't been able to hear? Speak to me now.

I am Your servant. Use me as You will. Do through me what You can convey to me to do, given my denseness? Help me to hear You clearly and correctly?

I ask in Jesus' name. What do You want me to know today, Father?

**Day 182**

Father God,

I can't imagine how frustrated You must be! You are *love*! And as love, You can and want to help us do everything. And we are so limited in our capacity to hear You—and it gets worse! We are so stupid, we don't want to hear from You! We are so gullible that some even believe that You no longer speak to us—what a bonus Satan got with that lie!

We are so self-centered, that we think that what we think and want is important! We must try Your patience to the max!

Father, I repent of believing that You don't speak to us. I repent of saying or thinking that I didn't want to hear from You. I repent of saying that I didn't want any gift or knowledge You wanted to give me.

Please forgive me and remove from me the consequences of those thoughts and actions? I ask in Jesus' name. What do You want me to know today, Father?

**Day 183**

Father God,

As I sit here in my little house, in my small town, on this small planet, I'm compelled to wonder why You took the time to create us. We are so ungrateful! You gave us more than our minds can handle. You gave us bodies we don't take care of. You let us have fine homes we don't appreciate, and cars to drive that we don't need. Then we sit and whine that we want nicer ones.

At this point, I admit that I have been ungrateful. I have failed to appreciate all that You are, and all that You have given to me. I have not thought about the time and effort You put in to do all this for all of us. Scripture says that You worked—which must have been something given Your abilities. I am so impressed. You have truly been a good and generous, Father, much better to me than I ever deserved.

You are too good! Forgive me for my ungratefulness, please? I ask in Jesus' name. What do You want me to know today, Father?

**Day 184**

Father God,

You are so good! Thank You for doing all the good things You do. Thank You for strengthening me and helping me get through today.

I need You so much today. I need Your strength. I need Your power! People think that I have patience but I don't. Inside I'm wound tight. Most of the time it doesn't matter, but when I blow, it really matters. I am so glad You take the time and have the patience to mess with me.

Please forgive me for losing it sometimes? Help me overcome myself? Forgive me for the times that I have hurt others? Please forgive me for not being what You hoped I would be? I want to be a delight to You, but I just keep messing up. Please help me? No one messes up as badly as me. Please forgive me when I'm a disaster?

I ask all these things in Jesus' name. I love You! What do You want me to know today, Father?

## Day 185

Father God,

Friends are necessary in life but they sure can be interesting! In my life I have known some doosies! In fact, I've known a lot of doosies! Most of my friends are singles now, which is weird since I'm married.

Speaking of contradictions, nearly everything in my life has contradicted the norm. Abnormal is normal for us. Maybe that's why I love the doosies! It's amazing that as much as we get wrong, I'm convinced that I got You right!

After all these years, I know that trusting You, relying on You and needing You are the wisest things I've ever done. I know that tithing in poverty, giving when we needed stuff, and trusting when there was no hope, have always worked out well for me.

Thank You for providing the day in and day out needs of my life! Thank You for letting us keep the house, own our cars, have phones, have TV and attend churches where they didn't throw out poor people! What do You want me to know today, Father?

**Day 186**

Father God,

When did You know that I would be alright? I was so messed up when I came back to You. I'm sure You must have carried me for awhile (and maybe still are). I had all those messed up ideas. Thank You for setting me straight! Thank You for not zapping me off the planet! I pulled some weird stunts when I first came back to You; I'm embarrassed to remember them; they were so stupid!

Now I'm watching my kids grow up and they are doing such stupid things—and are absolutely convinced that they are making wise choices.

Why did You give us free will? It has led to every problem or affected every problem in one way or another. We're like little kids in bumper cars. We just bump into each other all day long, each of us trying to do his or her own thing.

At least when I'm submitting to Your will, I'm staying on track and not getting hit so often. Thank You! Thank You for a safe track! What do You want me to know today, Father?

**Day 187**

Father God,

Thank You for Christian TV. Tonight, they are talking about doors shutting. I feel like You slammed the door on me, then locked it, and barred it, and welded it shut. The only problem I have with that, is that it was the only door! Are You about to blow a hole in the wall? I could use an exit here somewhere. I'm not seeing any windows, and if the power goes out it will be some kind of darkness in here.

Just so You know, You are free to break in here using any kind of tool You choose to break me out of this self-created cage. Yes, I'm aware You can DO anything; I'm just saying I won't mind how You break in, even if it scares me.

And if I ever get out, I want to be free, so please, could I have a set of invisible wings? I've been ground bound for so long! I want to soar with the eagles on the high places. I know all things happen when they are supposed to, but if You could speed things up, I'd appreciate it? I'm asking in Jesus' name. What do You want me to know today, Father?

**Day 188**

Father God,

You are the only one to whom I can't say, "Betcha can't guess what I'm thinking". You know my thoughts! And You know the intents of my heart. Lately those areas have done much better, but I still need Your help. I'm dealing with a whole lifetime of decades of wrong thinking! My head is full up with little lies, bad thoughts, and negative junk. I've let the TV, my friends, and movies all put junk in my head. I've sat and watched TV while saying, "This is junk, I shouldn't be watching it". It's like I poured a box full of puke and then dived in. It's that gross and stupid to let junk in me!

Help me use that power switch, please? Set me free from the trap? Keep me back from the temptation and deliver me from evil?

I need Your help on this one for sure. Help me cut off the junk-in part? I'm sick and tired of putting junk out. I ask in Jesus' name. What do You want me to know today, Father?

**Day 189**

Father God,

I want to thank You for good pastors. By that I mean all the pastors I've ever known. All of them have good hearts and a desire to help people. You used all of them to teach me, in one way or another, the things I needed to know. You are still teaching me through my pastor. Now I get to help share the load some and it blesses me so much that You trust me with that. In hoping I'm getting such a better look at the load a pastor carries and it is tremendous. You require so much of Your messengers! But I know they are blessed to be chosen.

Father, I ask You in Jesus' name, to give every pastor a gift of Your choice? Will You bless them as only You can? Will You ease their load in some way?

You are so wise to have given us shepherds. We are a stubborn bunch of goats and dumb sheep sometimes and we need the help. Thank You for being so good to us. What do You want me to know today, Father?

**Day 190**

Father God,

You are excellent in every way. You gave us Jesus as the example for our lives. Thank You for letting us know Your only son. Thank You for forcing Yourself to let him live on Earth so our debt could be paid. You could have stopped it. You could have sent angels to rescue him. History could have been rewritten, but You didn't do it, because You love us so much.

Jesus loves us, also, and was therefore willing to endure the pain to complete the work. As I read of his suffering again this week, I was so moved. He could have stopped it, too.

This planet could have been vaporized; but You both must have weighed the cost, and determined that we were worth saving. Thank You. No one will ever know how much it cost You to lose the ones who died when Noah and his family survived.

I am the least of those You spared and least worthy of the eternity You have promised me. I will work harder to be worthy of Your acceptance and love. What do You want me to know today, Father?

**Day 191**

Father God,

This has been a hard three days. I didn't know so much of me could hurt so much! I didn't expect it to be like this at all. I guess we never know what to expect in a work on us. A little adjustment, a little surgery and all will be better soon, but, oh, how the first three days can hurt! I have to say that I love it though. This body has given me fits for too long and it was time to cut out some of the problems—just like I love to go to the dentist. It may hurt for a minute while the needle goes in, but when the work is done all the pain is gone with the hole. I love the fact that You can and do fix our spiritual holes.

I love You for fixing all those tears in my heart. It had been getting pretty ragged when I found You. There may be someone else who has had a surgery this week of the spiritual kind, please help them as best You can and still accomplish the work? I ask in Jesus' name. What do You want me to know today, Father?

**Day 192**

Father God,

Thank You for churches!  T.D. Jakes just said, "We're better together than when we're apart".  It's so true.  As individuals we are all "parts" out of place.  But as a connected group of believers we complete each other.

We are all unique individuals.  We have our own DNA imprinted with our unique nature and personality.  By ourselves we are a tiny cog, useless on its own except as a paperweight.  But in the church, as part of the spiritual equipment used for the equipping of us, we are fully functional and fully actualized.  We are not the ministry, but we are needed to support one another.  If we each do the job assigned to us, the work will get done.

I remember when I just rode in the "church car".  But now I get to be part of the motor.  I love being part of the action.  I love supporting the ministry team.  And I love the roar of a good motor.  And I love You for changing our "job" from time to time!  Thank You so much!  What do You want me to know today, Father?

**Day 193**

Father God,

What a day! I never know who or what I'll encounter in a day's time! What a surprise. I didn't expect it at all.

And the bottom line is, You are still God and Jesus is still Lord of my life. Which brings me to the question, "What do I do now?".

Thank You for Your input of today. You have done so much for me over the years. Many times, I've faced a similar situation. You have seen me through them all. And always I have been grateful as I am now. I know that You will see me through this situation. I've seen hundreds of days now where I needed Your help and You have always been there for me.

It's so sweet to trust You and know You will always be there. You are too good to me!

Wonderful Father, thank You for seeing me through all the crises of my life! You are too good to me! What do You want me to know today, Father?

**Day 194**

Father God,

Remember the days when I was too busy to talk to You? I was so sure that I'd be fine on my own. Then I would fall on my face—literally! Remember the stitches on my nose at graduation? I remember when 300 people when "ouch" for me! My face healed but I'm not sure my pride ever has. Thank You for getting me through that one! Thank You for letting me kicked out of nursing school. That really hurt, but I needed to be humbled and You warned me to fast. Truly pride goes before a fall.

You are so good for me! Thank You for those humbling experiences and the scars! They help me remember that I can always get through whatever happens.

Today at this hour is the start of the rest of my life. I choose at this time to serve You, seek You and see Your hand for my good in every situation. I know that You love me and will not allow anything that is not for my eternal good.

Your purpose is bigger than my plans. Your goals are more important than my wishes. What do You want me to know today, Father?

**Day 195**

Father God,

They tell me that there are parts in an atom. They tell me there are bugs on bugs. (Somehow that is comforting; I don't know why.) It seems that everything is so complex now. Houses used to be made of wood and mud on dirt. Now we have footings, foundations, support beams, sub floors, floors and more. In our efforts to be more civilized we have added more components and more things that cost too much. We charge each other for things You made and gave us to enjoy! Then we look down on those who can't afford to pay for the things we "think" we should have. We put things over people ever day and brag about owning things! It is foolishness! Jesus told us in Matthew 24:35 that, "Heaven and Earth shall pass away, but my words shall not pass away."

Where do we get pride in things? We should be ashamed of putting our stuff over the people who use it. Forgive me for doing that, Father, please? And forgive me for claiming pride and ownership of things You own? I ask these things in Jesus' name. What do You want me to know today, Father?

**Day 196**

Father God,

Remember when I wanted to sing? Mom used to say I couldn't carry a tune in a bucket. I didn't know a melody from a harmony. And a key is something You used to open the door. I wanted to make beautiful music. And all I can do is muddle along.

Now I know that we can't all sing and it was a better tool for me to learn to type than play an instrument. My words are written, not sung, which is so good for me. I can write almost anywhere at anytime.

Thank You for giving my son the gift of song! He will do a much better job of it than I will! And thank You that his sister doesn't! Her gift is her big heart.

It constantly amazes me that You always give the right gift to the right person. We all have a gift, if we can find it.

Father, please show us our talents and gifts? Let me know what I do best? I ask in Jesus' name. What do You want me to know today, Father?

**Day 197**

Father God,

I ask You in Jesus' name to help me tonight. My head hurts; and my neck is popping. I'm so tired.

You have kept me safe and healed me too many times to count through these years. I've learned I can depend on You every time.

It's late and I got up so early. It's be a great day. It started bad and then went well, then bad, then good and now bad again. I love variety—but this is a little tiring!

No one can say my life isn't interesting. I seem to have constant upheaval. There is nothing boring about my story, as You well know. Are You preparing me for a really tough future? Some days I feel like I'm ready. I've gotten to be a really "tough lady" as a friend said.

Whatever You have for me, I'm glad to do it. Just being with You is so good that no matter what I'm doing I'm blessed to do it. Thank You for being so wonderful—especially in the midst of my "busier" days! What do You want me to know today, Father?

**Day 198**

Father God,

What will my obituary say? I wonder what the world will think of my pitiful efforts to do Your will.

We are such judgmental creatures. Will I be judged successful? Will You help me succeed at what You gave me to do? I'd rather be found successful by You.

I'm not a good wife or good mother. Have I done so poorly that my family called on You for help? I always wanted to do well. But it seems that if they needed You they were far more blessed. I remember asking You to help me be good at "mom" and "wife". I hope that despite whatever I did, You will fix it— or that I did what was right for them at the time.

I've always wanted to be a good Christian, but I'm not. Have I made others pray? It wasn't a goal, but if it was a result, I haven't totally wasted the trip.

Help me go out with the thought, "What can I do better?" Help me do better now? I ask in Jesus' name. What do You want me to know today, Father?

**Day 199**

Father God,

It's bedtime for me now but I wanted to say thank You one more time. You saw me through today, like You have so many other times, and I appreciate You so much. I am blessed beyond belief that You take so much time to listen to me and help me.

Some days I can hardly wait to see You and Jesus face-to-face. I know You'll be busy even then, but I'd love to say "thank You" in person (once I can get back on my feet). Until then I'll have to be satisfied with the hope that it will be soon.

I love the thought of Jesus' coming! I hope he astounds the world as they realize it was all true! I can somehow see You in my mind, sitting on Your throne and looking down beaming with pride on Your "Son".

It's getting close to the time when it will all end. I can see it all winding down. Thanks for telling us what will happen so we are expecting it!

What do You want me to know today, Father?!

**Day 200**

Father God,

I'm not being rebellious but sometimes I wonder why You made me the way I am. I'm under-tall, over-wide, and figure-challenged. I seem to have men's feet and a ten-year-old's hands. My friends say I have a big mouth but my dentists say it is small for a grown-up. And I started with red hair!

It makes me think of Mr. Potato Head toy. People have been known to laugh just to see me walk.

Other than the outside, I have problems, too. I speak too soon, think too fast, and act impulsively. Sad things are sometimes funny and funny things repulsive.

All of these things (and more) piled together have made my life hard in many ways. But I do thank You for them. If I hadn't had it hard, I'd have never needed You so much or experienced so much of Your love. It's been worth all of it, especially knowing that I don't have to take it with me to Heaven! What do You want me to know today, Father?

**Day 201**

Father God,

I ask You in Jesus' name to bless all my weird friends? Do what is best for the "stinker" we call "tea bag" because he wasn't worth much until he got in some hot water? Bless the Christian neighbor who collects beer mugs? Bless the "boy" who's wife is playing revolving door in his life? Bless the lady who over eats and blames her insulin? Bless "Pop", who has a bad name for every nationality? Bless the drunks who listen to Christian music all day? Bless the "bag man" with the bad back? Bless the "redhead who lost her kids because she won't work? Bless the lady with hives? Bless the girl who needs love so much that she keeps getting pregnant but misses out on the love? Bless the middle-aged "boy" who never mentally matured?

Do what is best for these and all my weird friends, please? Inside there isn't a bad heart among them, despite what the world may say about them. I ask these things in Jesus' name and ask that You forgive me my weirdness? What do You want me to know today, Father?

**Day 202**

Father God,

I remember the poem my mom used to say:

"For want of a nail, the shoe was lost;

For want of a shoe, the horse was lost;

For want of a horse the rider was lost;

For want of a rider the battle was lost;

For want of a battle the kingdom was lost;

And all for the want of a horseshoe nail." John Gower's

Confesio Amantis, 1390.


It reminds me to take care of the tiny details, but it also brings to my mind need so great that even tiny necessities are unaffordable.

For that reason, I ask You in Jesus' name to supply every ministry on this planet, which is going forth in Your name, and in obedience to Your will, with every single thing they need, no matter how tiny. Give the ministries funds, food, fun, vehicles, buildings, homes, and opportunities. Let them see and experience Your full and abundant provision as a testimony to those they are reaching out to with Your message. Let them be able to give thanks in their ministry for all You have done are doing for all of us? Give them what they need to win battles for You? I ask in Jesus' name. What do You want me to know today, Father?

**Day 203**

Father God,

Thank You for supplying all my needs! You are so good to us! You knew that a refrigerator would be needed and You gave us one for $40 just when we needed it!

So many times, I've gotten caught up in needs and focused on them instead of You. But I've never had a need go unmet! You always take care of us! It may come down to the wire but You always come through.

You are so faithful to be good to us. We don't realize most of the time what You do for us.

Please forgive me for not recognizing it when You do something for us? I should know by now that if we didn't have the money and it happened anyway, that You did it.

So many times, I've needed something and it was just there! Forgive me for dwelling on needs instead of on You. You are going to come through. That's all there is to it. You will supply my needs. Period. Forgive me when I don't acknowledge that? I ask these things in Jesus' name. What do You want me to know today, Father?

**Day 204**

Father God,

Someone said, "Coincidence is God's way of remaining anonymous."

It's so funny! You do it and we call it coincidence. I call a friend who was about to call me—coincidence? No, You know when we need a human ear to talk to so You gave us friends and whispered in our ear to call the other.

We run into someone we just met several times—coincidence? No, You know who we need in our lives.

Someone gets hurt and there's a doctor nearby—coincidence? No, the doctor was needed to care for someone.

My son gets thrown from a moving car—again—and lands on grass—coincidence? No, You are having extra angels protect him because You are calling him to serve You.

In all the little and big things of our lives You act to guide, provide and protect us.

Even as I needed money today and a friend left $10 in my car—You knew and supplied my need.

You are so awesome! What do You want me to know today, Father?

**Day 205**

Father God,

Stinky socks and messy clothes don't do a thing for my morale. But knowing that I have enough for a whole week at a time does! I remember when I only had the clothes on my back, and the set in the washer, for far too long.

Thank You for prosperity! Thank You for take-out food, cable TV, gas in my car, salad dressing and ketchup, and all the other things I couldn't afford for years. Especially thank You for my microwave and refrigerator and my computer.

I don't deserve comfort and ease and convenience any more than anyone on the planet, but You chose to bless me with those things. Thank You for being so awesome!

I love the fact that when they take up the offering, I know that I can put some in most of the time.

Thank You for being so kind and letting us have our comfortable lives and my very own recliner! What do You want me to know today, Father?

**Day 206**

Father God,

I deserved that beating!

I was telling You that I desired to know You and love You and take care of You, if I could. You've done so much for me. And then Holy Spirit said, "Inasmuch as You've done it unto the least of these, You've done it unto me."

If I truly want to show my love and devotion to You, I'll have to love and serve and care for those You send me. That includes my husband, my kids, my friends and my neighbors. And I can't leave any of them out! Because if I judge any of them unworthy, I'm saying You are unworthy, which is impossible!

Well, I'm busted! You know that I have not done well in that department. I've picked and chosen who I would love. Some days I must stink pretty badly!

Forgive me for not honoring Your creation when I judge others? Help me to see You in them and to serve them as I would You? I ask in Jesus' name. What do You want me to know today, Father?

**Day 207**

Father God,

Today I told a friend that You can't make today's decisions based on tomorrow's problems. I was trying to tell her to live for today so that she would not pay for things she doesn't need now, just because she might need them later.

How often do we do that? We proceed with things we don't need, just to save trouble later. The Bible clearly states that we should take no thought for tomorrow that the problems of today are sufficient. I see that in my life daily. Even as today's bare facts devastate me, I have no need to look ahead for more devastation. But yet so many see a possible problem and prepare for it, only to have it come to pass.

I am perplexed at that. Am I wrong to live for today and just try to handle today? Should I be saving and planning and worrying? I don't think so. None of those things are about You. I live so much of my life about me, none of it is eternal. Only You are eternal. Unless what I'm doing will make a difference in my eternity, I don't want to waste time doing it. Please help me to keep focused on You? I ask in Jesus' name. What do You want me to know today, Father?

**Day 208**

Father God,

Why is it that I count my life in numbers? All the moves, jobs, bosses, 20 some cars, four step-dads and six step-moms, four pregnancies, two children, 13 surgeries, 14 churches, 17 schools, 15 pastors, from hundreds to less than 10 friends, and one husband and one pink house. I've lost three moms, two grandmothers, three grandfathers, and many good friends to death.

All these numbers and it all adds up to one testimony that You saw me through it all. I've never been alone, although I thought I was when I walked away from You. Since June 16, 1975, I've known and seen Your hand on and in every event of my life. All the deaths and all the births were easier with Your help. All the losses and robberies were easier with Your love. All the gains and all the blessings were made better with Your blessing.

Every change that came with every decision was seen as necessary and was made easier with Your help. Nothing has happened that I didn't know I could count on You.

Your love still covers me and reassures me that I have a future and a hope with You. I'm so glad! What do You want me to know today, Father?

**Day 209**

Father God,

Will You fix me? I have several gifts that aren't blessings to others. I'd like to give back or alter some of them. I have a gift of being able to irritate people. Will You take it back, please? I have another gift of quick thought that causes me to interrupt people. Would You please keep my mouth shut while others are speaking? I have a gift of confrontation. Will You please help me do it in love? I have a gift for making excuses for my bad behavior. Will You please stop me and make me admit to it? I have a gift for thinking I'm always right. Will You please show me when I'm not? And I have a gift for not seeing any of my other negative "gifts". I'm thinking my giftedness is not such a good thing when I'm doing my will, my way.

Please forgive me and fix me? Help me to speak, act and be as You would have me be? I ask in Jesus' name. What do You want me to know today, Father?

**Day 210**

Father God,

It baffles me. When someone gets hurt, they blame You, Father, or sometimes the person who was there. There are so few times when a person deliberately hurts someone that it seems silly to say, "You did this to me."

Things just happen. And if they happen deliberately, Satan was behind it 99% of the time. Why would anyone think You could hurt someone? You are love. I know that sometimes You have to let things happen for our overall good, but You don't do anything for our harm.

Many things in my life have seemed overwhelming, but they weren't. They served to teach me better that You love me. I didn't like getting kicked out of two colleges, stitches in my nose at eighth grade graduation, having my car stolen by a roommate, or being judged unfairly. But all of it and worse was worth it because now I know You better, feel Your love more and see what a better person it has made me. I can understand other's pain so much better. Thank You for all the pain because it has taught me to love! What do You want me to know today, Father?

**Day 211**

Father God,

Why is it that we build a wall around ourselves to protect what we believe? If we found comfort in a verse, we anchor ourselves to it and build a case around it! But no verse stands alone. All of us need all of the verses to complete the message. No phrase by itself can be used. We are foolish if we think we have the whole truth! You said we won't! We are seeing and understanding through dark glasses.

Protect me from mindsets, Father? Keep me from false doctrines, please? Protect me from delusion and deception? Fill me full with the law of kindness and Your compassion? Let me be Your heart to this hurting world? Work through me to love the ones in pain? Help me see past the anger coming at me to the pain behind it. Help me speak as the balm of Gilead to the hurt in people?

I know this is asking a lot, but I see so much wrong and hurt out there. I'm asking in Jesus' name for the purpose of doing Your will better. What do You want me to know today, Father?

**Day 212**

Father God,

It is too early to be up, but I'm up again. I'm glad though because it gives me more time to be with You. Have I ever thanked You for taking the time to be with me? I do now. And thank You for letting me have time for You. Thank You, most of all, for always being there.

I never expected how much I would appreciate Your presence! Just to be able to call Your name and feel the change in the atmosphere is awesome. Holy Spirit in me will seem to fill every cell. And I know that I know that it is You. It sounds so strange to say it because it's a unique relationship, that of a flesh body and a spirit being. But I have a spirit and it flows with Your Holy Spirit. The result is so sweet. Thank You for letting Jesus come and suffer and die so I could enjoy this communion. Your communications are life to me and essential to my existence. Thank You for them! And I ask You, Father, in Jesus' name, to make Yourself real to everyone who doesn't know You as I do. What do You want me to know today, Father?

**Day 213**

Father God,

Help me see Your definitions?

From here I see treetops and a light pole with a reformer on it. If I defined my existence from that view, I'd have a pretty narrow world! But I do define my life in terms of what I know and have learned. It's stupid of me—please forgive me?

You are the creator of all things. Please help me to operate according to Your definitions and purpose?

I'm beginning to understand how limited and egocentric my world has become. I have an assignment given by You that exceeds what is in front of my nose. Today's work is essential, but tomorrow's must be prepared for also. My "view" is going to be changing and my knowledge base must keep increasing so I'll be ready for it.

My final petition today is that You will help me see when You are directing me so I won't miss it? I ask in Jesus' name for all these things. What do You want me to know today, Father?

**Day 214**

Father God,

In Jesus' name, I pray for our nations' leaders. I ask that You would work in them to bring them to full repentance. In each of their lives, work to show them Your power. Teach them to fear You so they can grow in wisdom and understanding? Help them to see the traps set for them by the enemy? Help them to see ways to seek You? Give them a hunger for scripture and the courage to use it?

Father, I ask You to work in and through all the citizens of our nation's capitol to reveal truth to them. Bring salvation to them in power! Let Your name be magnified and glorified on the lips of our elected officials. Let our nation return to its national heritage? Let the nations of Earth see the evidence that Your hand is on us. Let us find and express full repentance for the sins of our nation? I ask these things in Jesus' name. What do You want me to know today, Father?

**Day 215**

Father God,

We in America have done so many things wrong! It seems that we used our own reasoning to put ourselves in a mess. Our political system is a mess. Our welfare system is a failure. Our social security system is insecure. Our family structure is falling apart.

But despite all of that, You have always been a pillar we can lean on. You are safe and a secure harbor. You have been and always will be a place to hide from the storms of life. In the midst of it all—anger, evil, destruction and devastation—You are love. We can know that You will see us through whatever comes through at us. We will overcome with victory at the end!

Thank You for telling us the end of the story! Thank You for giving away the ending! It is a great security to know that we will overcome all that is thrown at us!

You are so awesome! You are sovereign! You rule in majesty and power! Hallelujah! What do You want me to know today, Father?

**Day 216**

Father God,

I hate to admit it out loud but I will. I have very little patience with the things I encounter daily. I like my yard kept nice. It isn't. I like my parking space, but I don't get it. I like to sit quietly sometimes; but I get interrupted. I think this may be a normal reaction; but I get really "riled up" as we used to say. I usually don't say anything, but underneath, I'm boiling. After all these years, why doesn't my family just do what I want them to do? Somehow, they should know a zillion little things that I like.

There's a catch here now that I really don't want to admit. I don't care what *they* want everyday. I believe this makes me the most selfish person I know. And I don't know how I got this way or have a clue on how to fix myself. But I'm sure this is not good, so, in Jesus' name I ask You to fix me, please? What do You want me to know today, Father?

**Day 217**

Father God,

When did I turn into an old battle axe? I was young and fun and happy once. And then I suddenly was bitter and angry and hard.

What were the little decisions that caused my personality to change? Was it when I decided not to hurt anymore, so I said, "I don't care" every time? Yes, that was part of it. Was it when I decided that I was more important than they? Yes, that, too. Was it when I began to dwell on the hurts I've received instead of the healer, Your son, Jesus? Yes, I think so.

I can't undo where I let myself go, Father. But with Your help, I can work on tomorrow. Please, in Jesus' name, help me to see others as more important to You? Help me to care? And help me to run to the healer, instead of saying, "I hurt", to everyone? And please for give me for taking so long to figure this one out? What do You want me to know today, Father?

**Day 218**

Father God,

One more time I don't have a clue what's really going on. I know that looking back at this I'll be glad I came through it but right now, I'm clueless. Could You drop me a hint? Something on the line of "I'm tweaking Your character here" or "I'm fixing an attitude" would do.

There it is! "No matter what the circumstances, what I feel or see, His word is working mightily in me". It's an old song, but the message is, You are working on me.

It's a little like going to the surgeon. If I ever saw the instruments, I might not go back! If I could pick my own instruments they'd all be rubber tipped and wouldn't work as well. So, one more time, I think I'll just close my eyes and say, "Have thine own way, Lord, have thine own way. Thou are the potter, I am the clay."

What do You want me to know today, Father?

[Adelaide A. Pollard, 1907. Pollard believed the Lord wanted her in Africa as a missionary, but she was unable to raise funds to go. In an uncertain state of mind, she attended a prayer meeting, where she heard an elderly woman pray, "It's all right, Lord. It doesn't matter what You bring into our lives, just have Your own way with us." At home that night, much encouraged, she wrote this hymn.]

**Day 219**

Father God,

Sometimes I wish I could be more like the cat. We maul her, rough her up, throw her out and yell at her. She doesn't mind.

Or like the dog. That dog lives to be talked to. She loves my husband as a one-man-fan-club. I've never seen the time she wasn't delighted to see him, even if it has only been one minute! She lives to see him and cries to get to him.

The cat on the other hand is just fine out on her own. When she wants attention, she's suddenly in my lap, despite what I'm doing. The dog is just there, continuously loving and waiting to be loved back.

I'm thinking now that You would rather have us be the constantly loving rather than occasionally demanding attention. I could learn from these critters, if I would. Help me learn from whatever You send my way, please? I ask in Jesus' name. What do You want me to know today, Father?

**Day 220**

**Father God,**

How soon we grow so old. I was a teenager yesterday. My children were born only minutes ago and their lives are gone from mine. They are setting their own courses now and how quickly they are learning.

It's amazing that yesterday's tragedies are lines on a memory page. Baby Valerie Jane, born premature on October 17, 1982 and died at 13 days. Yesterday's blessings have also passed quickly. I bought a brand-new house and already it's 30 years used.

And through it all, friends have come and gone. Have I been a good friend? I hope so, but I'm sure I've failed some. Please, Father, help me to help others in their tragedies and rejoice in their joys? Help me to be a friend they can count on to laugh with and cry on? Help me to show Your heart to them when they sorrow and when they laugh? And send me to the ones who need a friend the most? I ask in Jesus' name. What do You want me to know today, Father?

**Day 221**

Father God,

Thank You for my treasures! I love them so much.

I remember being eight years old and falling in love with babies. I didn't know it would be 24 years before I brought one home from the hospital. Through the years You let me have "borrowed treasures" and I'm so glad. I cared for so many other children that my own were easy. If my last name hadn't been Love, my daughter Melody would have been named Treasure! Thank You for sparing her that! Of course, I didn't know that I would have absolutely no help with them, but You did. Thank You for making them normal, despite my influence.

I'm so glad that my treasures have been people instead of things. You saw to it that I didn't have many things—possessions or accomplishments, which is good since I messed up most things I did anyway. And I'm grateful that my children have always been and always will be my greatest treasures, and that I knew that before they were born. Thank You for letting me enjoy every day of our lives together.

Now that they are on their own, and I can't be there for them, will You bless my "treasures"? I ask in Jesus' name. What do You want me to know today, Father?

**Day 222**

Father God,

You are so impressive. I knew I wanted to speak to that lady and You brought her to my door! Thank You!

Thank You for all the times You have sent the right person at the right time to help me! You are so over-whelmingly able! <u>You are the man</u> as we used to say—meaning You do what no one can!

Just when I needed a friend You brought the right person to me—four times now for four different seasons of my life! You know me best and that was no easy task!

Now I see You sending me to help others with a little word of encouragement or a prayer and I think I'm more blessed than they are. I want so much to give back some of those times when You directed a human to help me. I'm not very able so it's a thrill when a little prayer is all they need! Thank You for letting me do my little bit! What do You want me to know today, Father?

**Day 223**

Father God,

I deleted what I just wrote because history has changed since I wrote it. The event I prayed about didn't happen. So many of the events I have planned have not happened and I know it's been because *I* planned them. Why is it that if an event seems good to do, I go ahead and do it without asking You if I should do it? Just because it seems good doesn't mean that it is good.

I've known churches that were doing great so they built a great building, only to find out it wasn't so great. I've known people who lost their life savings on a business venture that they didn't understand how to run. I have made countless plans and seen Your hand as You shut every door.

The plans keep coming, which tells me that the brain keeps working, whether or not the heart is listening. It seems that we humans think we know best what to do for us. Isn't that silly? We were created by You, why wouldn't we ask You what is best for us to do? I'm sorry I've been so stupid about it. Please forgive me? And *tell me* what *You* would like me to do? I ask in Jesus' name. What do You want me to know today, Father?

**Day 224**

Father God,

I don't know why You brought our friend into our life. He's mentally challenged to the point of being a full-time resident at a care facility. Yet You gave him to us and declared us to be his family.

You truly do "place the solitary in families" (Psalm 68:6). It has been a trial so many times to have him visit here. Every holiday he is part of what happens. And yet he calls us "home".

And then there is the friend who comes to use us as sounding board. He chooses to come here to vent. We are often frustrated by him, but we know he needs us. It's good to know we can be what someone else needs, even if it costs us something.

I'm sure we are like that to You. Messing up Your house, eating Your spiritual food, taking Your time and always wanting something; we must try Your patience. But if I didn't have You to come home to, where could I go? I had lost my own family when I found You.

They let me go. I'm a spiritual nut; they think. It probably is true. I'm in love with an invisible being, whom I talk to daily, and try to follow the practices of a book written over 2000 years ago. I don't mind one bit what they think. As long as I have You, I'm good. Thanks for letting me come home! What do You want me to know today, Father?

**Day 225**

Father God,

Some days I think these recliners were not such a good idea. I'm grateful for them, truly, but I'm a little too attached to mine. I know that I fought for a comfortable seat for the first time in my life—I'm too short for many chairs, but this one may fit a little too perfectly. It's a little like I used to do church. I got so settled into my "place" that I could only see from one perspective. And I would miss the great stuff happening behind me!

Part of me never grew up, I'm afraid. I still "wanna see" and "wanna do" whatever is going on. For years I sat in my seat and stretched my neck but wasn't part of very much. I'm glad You finally got me out of my comfort zone and that good seat! It's so much better to be part of what's happening. I love the fact that when I pray it makes a difference. I know it does because You said it would. I'm glad You told us to pray.

Thank You for letting me "play, too" (or should I say "pray", too), and for this great recliner when I get home for my quiet time with You! What do You want me to know today, Father?!

**Day 226**

Father God,

Thank You for good neighbors!  And thank You for so many other things I thought of today:

> only one cat owns us
>
> we have only one dog
>
> only one house to care for
>
> only one phone line at home
>
> one wonderful air conditioner
>
> that wonderful dish washer
>
> only one spouse
>
> one small town to cross daily
>
> frozen cold drinks in the summer!

At my age the little things get more and more precious.  I remember when big things were all I wanted.  Just now I'm quite happy in my recliner and talking to You.

I think I'm most grateful that You didn't give me too much money.  If I had had more money, I'd have more "stuff" to take care of and less time to enjoy this.

You know me better than I do and gave me just what I needed!  Thank You, Father! What do You want me to know today, Father?

**Day 227**

Father God,

Every day I need a new way to praise You. You are worthy of every word, every thought, and every deed. You are worthy of all time, all credit and all glory.

I sit in frustration because my vocabulary doesn't do justice to the immensity of Your being. Your existence is to love. I can't process the magnitude of such a task.

For You it is as easy as breath. Because You are love, You don't have to work at it or make a decision to do it. It is Your nature, not just a part of it.

I'm encouraged by the fact that I'm made in Your image. I have hope that someday I may love as You do.

Will You renew me? Will You take me back to my childhood, when I trusted and loved freely? Will You heal the scars that have bound my heart and mind, and kept me from giving love freely? I ask in Jesus' name.

What do You want me to know today, Father?

**Day 228**

Father God,

I am so lost without You. I am in a maze of loneliness without You. I find myself encompassed about with silence. All of my days I have had the sound of people. Now I am surrounded by their absence.

I didn't know I could be so alone and be okay. There's never been a time when I was so free of humans.

The change is immense, but the price is small. I am so enjoying the total freedom to call Your name and feel Your presence.

You are so good to me! You are so precious! I'd rather have You than all the people I've known. Being with You builds me up; You make me better in every way.

Thank You for letting me have You as my best friend. Thank You for letting me experience Your love. You are so good in every category! Awesome, wonderful, glorious, God.

Thank You for all that You are and do. What do You want me to know today, Father?

**Day 229**

Father God,

What is a hero in Your eyes? I've been watching hero stories on TV because of the Fourth of July programming. It makes me wonder. We call someone a hero who saves a life.

Is that Your definition? Do You recognize those who save our flesh? Or do You recognize those who preach the message that brings us to belief? Do You recognize martyrs? Or is Your hero the prayer warrior who fights from the knee? Is Your hero the Sunday school teacher? Or is it the door to door evangelist? Do You recognize the healing ministries?

Do You acknowledge the ones who protect us and our children? I'll probably never be a hero, I know, but someday, if You are willing, I'd love to meet someone who is a hero in Your eyes. Until then, will You please bless those heroes You know by meeting all of their needs? I ask in Jesus' name. What do You want me to know today, Father?

**Day 230**

Father God,

Have You noticed, of course You have—duh, but humans are groupies by nature. We get ourselves into groups, clics, clubs, churches, organizations and sets as soon as we get old enough.

More than anything we want to be "part of" a group. Some of us, me included, want to be leaders. For me, it proves I'm not so smart. For others, it is their destiny.

At the root of it all is the desire for commonality and acceptance. We want to look like the herd of sheep, even if we were born a goat!

Father, I'm sure that I want to be one thing these days—what You want me to be! If You can use this old goat You may do what You want with me, even if it means being the scape goat, because someone has to take out the trash. Your will be done, Father, in me. What do You want me to know today, Father?

**Day 231**

Father God,

I'm convinced that a self-cleaning house would be the ideal home. I would make the walls and floors with self-washing features disguised as fountains. Then the furniture could shake itself to rid itself of dust. Carefully hidden vacuums would clean the air and collect cat and dog hair; then clean themselves.

In the ideal home all dishes would be disposable and all food self-heating or cooling.

Yards would be hardscaped with limited areas of plastic grass.

It's a nice vision isn't it? And I'm truly not lazy. I just don't like doing housework. Not doing it won't make it go away, though.

Which brings me to my point. I ask You in Jesus name to help me set this house up so it is the easiest house on the planet to keep clean, and give me a desire to clean it? That's the miracle I need today. What do You want me to know today, Father?

**Day 232**

Father God,

I CAN'T DO THIS! I am absolutely, positively, totally incompetent when it comes to running my own life! I have made decisions in full confidence my whole life and the result is complete crash!

I need Your help! I can't continue on my own.

At this rate I will soon implode, explode or otherwise self-destruct!

I am beyond human help. I am without resource, without hope and without comfort.

You are the only one who can help me and it may take all of Your resources and a big chunk of Your time. I've made a colossal mess of my life that only You could untangle.

I don't deserve it; but if You will, would You, could You, please, unravel, untangle, and unwind my disaster and straighten out my life?

I ask this in Jesus' name and throw myself on Your mercy. What do You want me to know today, Father?

**Day 233**

Father God,

As an act of my will, I set aside my day. I hope that <u>You</u> have had a good day. I hope You had fewer whiners, fewer gimme-prayers, fewer fix-somebody-else-prayers, and fewer demands on Your time overall.

I hope You had lots of praise and thanks, lots of adoration and more than average worship.

I hope things went smoothly in all Your categories.

And Father, I ask You in Jesus' name to forgive me for whining, praying gimmies, and asking You to fix others. I know that You know my situation, know what I need, and are fully capable of fixing others, and knowing when to do it. And for my part, I declare that to my knowledge You are the best, most worthy, able and capable being that exists! You are God!

I love, adore, worship, want, need and desire to know You better every day of my life! What do You want me to know today, Father?

**Day 234**

Father God,

Please, in Jesus' name, apply the blood of Jesus to my situation? Cover my home, finances and work situation with His blood. I need my life covered completely for protection, cleansing, restoration and renewal.

I need the complete work of the cross in and on my life.

And Jesus, thank You for that work! Thank You for suffering and giving up Your blood in agony for me. Thank You that my healing is complete and paid for by You! Thank You that I can be forgiven, healed emotionally and restored physically.

Thank You, Holy Spirit, for being my teacher, confidant, healer, and counselor. Without You, I'd be adrift at sea with no sail or rudder. Father, I honor You and appreciate You for enabling the reconciliation of mankind to Yourself. We don't deserve to be reconciled to You—but we need restoration and thank You for allowing Jesus to be the means of reconciliation. What do You want me to know today, Father?

**Day 235**

Father God,

I love the way You encourage me by having something happen that matches what I need just as I think of it or recognize a need. It is so incredibly not-coincidental that You do those things! Especially now when I'm feeling the need to be encouraged and You keep sending encouragement.

I can't believe You love me so much!

I like trusting You. I have a sense of great peace that only You could have given me. It is a welcome change for me. I love letting You lead in my life. What a difference it makes to trust You with everything. Just to do what I can and then let You have it.

Thank You! Thank You for teaching me the peace that comes with trusting You.

You are so awesome! Incredible, wonderful God! You are so good! What do You want me to know today, Father?

**Day 236**

Father God,

Today is a first for me. I'm stepping into new territory. Since I have not done this before, will You please guide my steps?

I am so unprepared for this but know that somehow I will get through. My only confidence is in Your leadership. You have brought me to the edge of the nest. Now I must trust that, as You shove, my wings will take over.

The edge is scary. I've never been afraid of heights, but I've never jumped more than 20 feet either. Would You send a big wind just as I jump? I'm not much of a flyer either. Scripture says I can trust in the shadow of Your wings. Would You please fly overhead or be my net beneath?

These are lousy metaphors for what is really happening, but You know my thoughts. You know what is happening. So, I ask in Jesus' name that You work through me to do what needs done so You are glorified? What do You want me to know today, Father?

**Day 237**

Father God,

Dirty windows are bugging me. I never did like a dirty window and my house is full of them. I have always kept them clean but with the knee issues I kept having for so long, these windows look pretty bad. I can't see clearly through them, even though I seldom try.

This brings me to that scripture:

1Cor. 13:11-12 "When I was a child, I spake as a child, I understood as a child, I thought as a child: but when I became a man, I put away childish things. For now we see through a glass, darkly; but then face to face: now I know in part; but then shall I know even as also I am known."

I'm not sure that I'm seeing clearly these days. Based on what my peers are saying, my windows are dirty. Am I missing You somehow? Am I seeing what I want to see and not what You are trying to show me? Have I missed the road by looking through dirty thoughts and misleading goals, motives or purposes?

Would You adjust my vision, please? Will You fix the goals, motives and purposes I'm following? Will You please point out the errors of my way? I'm a mess here, and I need some heavenly window cleaner. I ask in Jesus' name. What do You want me to know today, Father?

**Day 238**

Father God,

It is good to know that we were created! It is good to know that You have everything under control!
You are truly so good to us! Thank You for prophets who let us know what to expect! As I look at weather trends, it would be easy to wonder at what is happening; but it is obvious that it is just all part of the plan!

Thank You for the plan! You are so generous to let Your creation in on the future. You didn't have to give us a clue and could have left us to stumble in the dark! Thank You for all the clues!

I know that in Your wisdom You couldn't tell us the whole sequential story or we wouldn't do our part. It is so good to know that You will do Your part and we will do our part, if we are in You will.

In Jesus' name, I ask You to show me my part? Let me know what to do, so I will be there for the reward, and the end of the story? What do You want me to know today, Father?

**Day 239**

Father God,

You are so good to me! Thank You!

I'm totally indebted to You. I love Matthew 6:12, "And forgive us our debts". Since Jesus was telling us how to speak prayer to You, he is reminding us that we owe You so much. Jesus himself paid the debt for our sins. We owe You for that. We owe You our lives.

Thank You for that! And Father, I do ask in Jesus' name for Your forgiveness. I have not paid You anything in return. I have not given anything for the great debt that was paid for me.

The word says I was "bought with a price", but I have not been a good purchased servant. Please God, help me to hear You clearly, study and understand Your word fully, and comprehend Your will for me precisely? I want to be a servant well worth the price paid. As a sinner, I defiled the life You gave me. Help me not to defile the name of Christian which You have given me? I ask these things in Jesus' name. What do You want me to know today, Father?

**Day 240**

Father God,

Thank You for giving me the opportunity to apologize! I am so grateful that You let me make it right even though I didn't say it. It was good to see the touch of Your hand on a heart that had been wounded.

Please forgive me for all the times I did the hurting and didn't apologize? I need to see when it is me that speaks out wrongly. Help me realize when I've said something that I shouldn't have?

You are so good to heal our emotions! Thank You for healing mine! Thank You for enabling and equipping me to freely forgive and fully apologize for myself and others!

I know that for years I could not forgive. Please help me to forgive those who have hurt me? Especially the ones I thought I forgave but didn't? I ask all these things in Jesus' name, so I may be a better person for You. What do You want me to know today, Father?

**Day 241**

Father God,

Thank You for not giving us instant replay! I would hate to have to relive someone else's mistakes so they could see it again. This seems weird, I know, but You who sees all, know we don't want to redo. I've asked You before to just let me "do over", but if I did, it would just put others through the mess again as well.

So…. Thank You once again for not answering that prayer with a "yes"!

And thank You for saying "no" to all the other silly prayers—like "make me taller/smaller/prettier" and many others. I'm so glad prayers aren't machines—put one in, pull out a product. Thank You for not allowing those things that would hurt us now or down the line.

You are so wise and so responsible! Thank You for saying "no" so often! What do You want me to know today, Father?

**Day 242**

Father God,

Help me find my identity in You? Help me define myself by Your descriptors? Let me be found in You?

I am not my accomplishments. I am not my goals. I am not my education. I am not my work experience.

All of these things have been tools to shape me and, in many ways, have warped me. But in the end, when I stand up for judgment, I want to hear "well done". For that reason, I give You now all these things in my history and I surrender me.

Whatever I am today is not what I will be. And when this time is over, I want to be someone You want to see. I need Your approval; I don't need or want human approval.

If there is anything in me that diminishes Your glory, will You cut it out? Will You lay the knife to my heart? Will You remove any part of me that demeans You? And will You work in me until I'm a lantern for Your light? I ask in Jesus' name. What do You want me to know today, Father?

**Day 243**

Father God,

Thank You for day jobs! So many times, we hear, "Don't quit Your day job". For most of us, the day job is our means of living day in and out. It is Your method of provision and presenting ministry opportunity.

Help me to remember that my workplace is my mission field? Help me to recognize ministry opportunities when I see them? Help me remember that ministry isn't contained in a church building?

It blesses me that You gave us churches so we can fellowship with "fellow" soldiers. I love to share war stories with my comrades. But it is such a greater good to war for the souls of the lost and help heal the wounded. Thank You for great nights and battle glories!

My career will never be my fulfillment, but it will always be my battleground. Thank You for that.

In Jesus' name I ask these things, and that You be my commander. What do You want me to know today, Father?

**Day 244**

Father God,

Please bless the person I'm waiting for? Give then organizational skills, time management awareness, and speed? Bless them with consistency of movement, less distractions, and fewer aches? Give them a healthy body, good eyes, good ears, and a motivation to never keep people waiting?

I know this is a selfish prayer, but would You please give me the ability to accept this wait as part of Your plan for me? Will You help me imagine that this delay is keeping me from an unpleasant event? That would be a nicer round of thought than that nasty thought I usually get. And will You forgive me the nasty thoughts?

And forgive me for making You wait while I grow up? I'll get there someday, just as this person will. Help me realize it may not be their fault?

I ask these things in Jesus' name. What do You want me to know today, Father?

**Day 245**

Father God,

It's two days until…

It's 24 days until…

How easy it is to get caught up in "that which is to come"! Now is my only opportunity to do well in this minute. If my focus is always on "when", I will miss "now" and wonder how nothing was done. You have all my "whens" in Your hand and under control. I make a decision today to live with open eyes and ears for today. I want to be Your hands today. And when "when" gets here, I will be Your hands then as now.

Until "when", will You please teach me how to better do "today"? Will You bring to my attention opportunities to love? Will You speak through me to hurting hearts and wounded spirits?

I fix my attention on You in this moment so I can be Your vessel of healing. Help me?

I ask these things in Jesus' name. What do You want me to know today, Father?

**Day 246**

Father God,

I will base my life on my tomorrows, not my yesterdays. It comes to mind that if I can focus on my future, my goals and on improving myself, I'll do better than if I spend my time regretting the past.

My yesterdays have been the learning experiences that have brought me to today. I loved them by following my nose and going to what interested me. Now, with Your help, I want to live to become what You need me to be. I would rather spend my time preparing for the "final exam" on judgment day, than worrying about the test I failed yesterday. I will work to know the scriptures and learn the things You need me to know.

Yesterday is gone. The pains of yesterday are history. I release them to You. I can't go fix the test, so I refuse to carry the guilt any longer. I give it up now.

Father, I ask in Jesus' name that You help me "study" for the "final exam"? What do You want me to know today, Father?

**Day 247**

Father God,

"Oh, what joy is mine…leaning on the everlasting arms". The songwriter must have learned to trust You! I feel the joy, even in my situation. The outcome of this week will greatly affect my future. I'm so glad my outcomes are in Your hand.

Because You are working all things for my good, even the suspense is joyful. I love to watch You work! It's less fun when I'm the one doing the squirming, but it's okay. I feel a little like a little kid whose shirttail is nailed to the floor. I'm trying to move but am not going anywhere! I'm trying hard though, and when You pull that nail out, I'll probably burst out the door. Would You please trip me inside, so I will slow down before I can fall down the steps? By that I mean, will You direct my exuberance?

When the hindrance is about to be removed, will You put on ankle weights—to make me go slow and remind me daily that I still need You? I ask in Jesus' name. What do You want me to know today, Father?

**Day 248**

Father God,

Thank You for my feet! I've got great feet. They are too wide, the instep and arch are too high, and comfortable shoes are not made for me. I am blessed with the opportunity to buy great insoles in a country that is material rich.

These feet of mine are sturdy, practical, reliable and funny looking. My fat little toes are stubby and fully functional. Those toes give me great balance. And thank You for protective toenails. My feet are so unique that I have to wear ugly shoes.

It's good to know that I'll never have to worry about wearing pretty shoes again. It's good to know that my feet will last as long as I do. Thank You for my reliable transportation!

As part of the whole body You chose for me, it is evident that You have given me a perfect shell. You knew before I was born what I would need. It is so good that I didn't get the wrong one! You have helped me stay humble and this body is one of Your great tools! Thanks! What do You want me to know today, Father?

**Day 249**

Father God,

Thank You for not letting me do all the things I don't want to be now. I remember wanting to be so many things. I was so sure of myself and so cocky. But You in Your wisdom, have assigned me a lesser role. I would never have been able to do all those things.

Thank You for not letting me have the things that would have hurt me.

I love You for the fact that I can look back and see Your hand in everything I've been through!

You are so good to help me so much. Nothing is done without Your knowledge. Nothing can happen outside of Your will.

Knowing that You have all things under Your control is so great! You are the answer-holder, solution-giver, and problem-solver! You are the one to turn to who will always do what is best for me! Thank You! What do You want me to know today, Father?

**Day 250**

Father God,

Now is the beginning of the rest of my life. Sometimes I forget that "now" is my "opportunity". Now is my "chance". Help me to live so I don't look back someday and say, "I missed my opportunity", or "chance passed me by"? Help me to be aware that now may be my only chance and I must take options seriously?

You have been so gracious to me. You have repeatedly rescued me and reversed circumstances. In this moment You are again in charge of my destiny. I'm so glad it's You. I would hate to think that I'd be in charge today. The best part is that You are all-knowing! You know what's ahead and where I will complete my assignment.

My only task is to decide in this moment to turn loose, hand You the reins and enjoy the ride. Help me enjoy the ride? The view is glorious if I can look to the view instead of the road. I ask in Jesus' name. What do You want me to know today, Father?

**Day 251**

Father God,

All of my life I've eaten every day that I wanted to. I've always had a place to live. I've had cars or the ability to walk. I've had family and friends. I've had jobs or You have provided in other ways.

Today I honor You for all that! It was Your choice to give me a great family. We have always loved despite our struggles. We always had enough food although I lost unnecessary weight a few times. I've been able to get to work and church and school. Miles of walking never hurt me.

You have been there when my feet hurt, my cars broke down, my cupboard was empty and all You have asked for is my thanks!

Today I thank You for years of provision, solutions, rescues, and friendship! You are a generous and righteous father. I thank You and appreciate You so much! What do You want me to know today, Father?

**Day 252**

Father God,

Honor and glory, power and praise to Your name. Your name is above all names. Your name is exalted far above all! You are the only God. Your name is full of power and glory. Your name is majestic and full of awe. You alone are worthy of Your name.

Great, glorious, and grand; Your glory exceeds our imagination. Your power is greater than the sum of all powers. Your might is invincible.

No force can withstand the power of Your name. No enemy can conquer Your might. No being is Your equal. Beyond limitation or containment, You live outside the frameworks we build for You.

Your glory exceeds the glory of a thousand suns in one! Your light pierces the darkness and cleanses the soul. Your love heals the spirit. No one is Your equal. No one is Your peer. No one compares to Your glory! Great is Your name. Holy, holy, Lord God Almighty. What do You want me to know today, Father?

**Day 253**

Father God,

Our talks are an exchange of thoughts that mean little to others, but are life and breath to me.

Your love is a wrap of tender compassion spoken only to my heart.

Mercy from Your hand comes without judgment or admonition.

You have a spot in my being that is expanding beyond my spirit and filling my soul. I surrender both spirit and soul with joy. Neither singer nor poet could describe the effect Your love has on me. Words are invalid and useless to define the change Your gifts have worked in me. The thought of Your touch fills me with anticipation of great joy. I settle into Your love with ease and full trust, knowing that You will protect me.

Read my heart, hear my heart's desire, let me be with You, beloved Father. You are my life. What do You want me to know today, Father?

**Day 254**

Father God,

 Outward, standing, strong to the world,

 Inward, kneeling dependent on You,

 You are my strength.

 You are my source.

 I have no one I trust but You. None but You are absolute, guaranteed or reliable. You never fail, run out, run off, disappear, give in, give up or surrender. Your supplies are endless, perfect, complete, flawless and always appropriate. Your strength is unfailing, never weakened, never bound and ample for every task.

 As is everyday, today I will see Your power manifested and Your strength revealed. Today I will feel Your love in a higher dimension, a new depth, a new width and a new height. You are not limited to my three-dimensional world. You are not limited to my concept of reality. You are not containable or limitable, nor do You cease. You are God Almighty and there is no other! What do You want me to know today, Father?

**Day 255**

Father God,

For every time I failed You, I ask Your forgiveness.

For every time I denied You, I ask Your forgiveness.

For every time I didn't speak up for You, I ask Your forgiveness.

I am a sinner. I have sinned in failing and denying You. I have sinned in not speaking up for You.

You have made me, blessed me, and given me all that I need. All You ask is that I confess You before men. I have failed to do that. I desired to be cool and in doing so, did not confess You. I have misled people by my practices.

Rebuke me, oh God, that I may learn and not continue in sin? Restore my soul and create a right spirit within me? In all my ways I desire to glorify You. In all my ways I desire to serve You and magnify Your name. Please heal me and forgive me?

I ask in Jesus' name. What do You want me to know today, Father?

**Day 256**

Father God,

Tonight, I can't think of any new ways to praise You. That's a shame because You are worth every good word a thousand times over.

You are worth first ideas and full expressions. You are worth creative nuances.

Your name is worth descriptive phraseology and colorful adjectives.

Father, Your character deserves flowery praise in skillfully written stanzas. Your being should be readily comprehended, and easily explained to those who don't know the extent of Your uniqueness.

You are the superlative expression in all colloquialisms and native tongues. Affirmatives and interjections should be used for emphasis and strengthening of mundane word groups to describe You.

Praise should be a genre of its own, developed to suit Your pleasure.

I am a poor writer for I can't think of a new way to say, "You're the best of all and greater than all known beings!" Please forgive me for my clumsiness and awkwardness? What do You want me to know today, Father?

**Day 257**

Father God,

Sometimes I want to write bad country songs to You. Not bad bad—just I'm a poor singer bad. I'd use repetitive phrases and whiny noises to tell You how good You are. Not because it's what You deserve, but because it's all I know.

Maybe You'd be tickled and maybe You'd groan, but I'll bet there's somebody doing it right now. I think we all try to find ways to express what we feel to You.

It seems to me that even a bad rhyme is better than no rhyme, if it's an attempt to praise You.

Anyway, I'm not writer, but if You'd pass on these ideas I'd appreciate it:

"Have I told You lately that You love me…

"Nobody loves me like my God loves me…

"You touch my heart…clean my spirit, heal my soul…

'He loves me, He loves me always…

"You are cooler than my horse, cooler than my car, faster than my computer…

'Until we meet in heaven, take my heart for now…

(Just ideas, You know!) What do You want me to know today, Father?

**Day 258**

Father God,

I'm sorry. Today was such a waste; I spent the whole day focused on what I thought could/should/would happen. Nothing happened! If I had decided to spend the day working, or reading the word or even helping someone else, how much more profitable it could have been.

But even these thoughts don't change now. Now is my moment. Now I recognize that my life is in Your hands to do with as You will. Now is my time to turn loose of what will/might/should or could happen. I can't analyze, decide, figure out or cause one thing to change. All I can do is continue to seek You and continue to praise You. I repent of my thoughts. I surrender to You my future. I relinquish all control and all plans for the outcome.

You are LORD, You are able and You are capable. I praise Your holy name. What do You want me to know today, Father?

**Day 259**

Father God,

Thank You for meeting with me. I am so blessed that You spend time with me. You are so sweet and good to me! In all things and at all times, You are my source of strength and power. You always give me just what I need, just when I need it. You are my supply, my storehouse, and my provider. You dole out the needs of my life as they are needed. It is so good to know that my needs will be met because You planned for my provision. Just as a good army plans for the provisions for its troops, You have ordered ahead for the housing, money, clothing, and transportation needs I will have. My language has no word to describe that but "cool"! You thrill my heart and build my spirit every time I see Your provision. Since You have always come through, I know You always will come through! You are so great! What do You want me to know today, Father?

**Day 260**

Father God,

In the strife, in the battle, in the field, and in the office, You are there! You await our call with eager anticipation. Like a good parent, You have sent us out to learn for ourselves. You look for our call and watch for our visit. You are so wise and You know that until we come to You, we will not hear You. It must be frustrating to You, the holder of all knowledge, to be ready to help and not be asked to help. I'm so sorry. How I wish I'd started asking for help 30 years ago! My story would be so much different now.

Today I open my mind and heart and say, "Tell me! Tell me whatever You know that will help me have a better life so I can come home with a good report." I surrender my "wants" and "don't want to-s" to You. I set aside my ideas about how things should be done. Speak to me—I ask in Jesus' name. What do You want me to know today, Father?

**Day 261**

Father God,

There truly is life and death in the power of the tongue. How quickly our words bring us down! We throw them out as freely as we breathe, but the consequences can be so costly.

We injure ourselves and others in our casual conversations. Our little witticisms and comments cut to the bone of the human spirit. We are entrapped by our own words. Ecclesiastes 10:14 says, "A fool also is full of words". Proverbs 29:11 says, "A fool uttereth all his mind: but a wise man keepeth it in 'til afterwards."

Burn these scriptures to my tongue, Father. Teach me to hear much and speak little.

And, Father, please forgive me for all the cutting remarks I've made about others and the judgments I've spoken? I need You so much; please don't hold this against me? I ask these things in Jesus' name. What do You want me to know today, Father?

**Day 262**

Father God,

If I could choose my life again, would I? (Assuming I chose any part of this!) It's a moot question of course, but it makes me think.

In this life I've been abused, assaulted, robbed, neglected, abandoned, used, and more—all to some degree. Through it all I've learned to trust You, to call for Your help and so much more. I've gained the ability for compassion, love, patience, strength, trust, mercy and grace.

I must not have chosen this—I would have chosen comfort, ease and plenty! And I would have learned to be selfish, self-centered and greedy!

Thank You for choosing a life for me that would help me better prepare for an eternal life! I would hate to go through eternity thinking only of myself; it's bad enough the way I am now. Thanks for taking some of the bad out of me and making me better! What do You want me to know today, Father?

**Day 263**

Father God,

You alone know the plans You have for me. You know the job You are preparing me for. You know what I need to know to be fully equipped. You are my advisor, counselor, and guide.

When I am all alone on the vast blue sea, You surround me with tranquility. You cover me with shade in the midst of the treacherous desert. You anoint me with oil when I am parched and dry. Your presence is like cool water to this thirsty soul.

My life's breath is dependent on Your provision of air. When I can't face the day for the terror of the coming storm, You wrap me in arms of love and sustain me. When the wind begins to buffet me about, You carry me.

I have no life without You! I have no hope, no future—nothing without You. Please don't ever leave me? In Jesus' name, I plead—never leave me? What do You want me to know today, Father?

**Day 264**

Father God,

Today I experienced the compassion of others. I needed help and had to ask for it. They met my needs in kindness and mercy. I hated the asking. I'm a proud and independent woman and just hated to have to ask. I had to ask strangers. How painful it was to have to ask. But they responded without harassment. Without challenging my need and without judgment, they provided. I'm so grateful! Thank You for servants of mercy and givers of grace! Thank You for sending me to a place where I could get my needs met.

You are my provider. You have always been and always will be my provider. But sometimes we have to let people help us. How I hate it when I need another person to do for me! But I remember that even Jesus couldn't do everything. Women prepared that last meal. Women prepared him for burial. Women came to the tomb. He was regularly served by them in a culture that did not value them. I am thankful that I was helped. I must trust that the means of help was sent by You. Thank You for all the times You have provided for my needs, by whatever means You used. What do You want me to know today, Father?

**Day 265**

Father God,

An end is always a beginning. I wrote that to remind myself that what I see may look like an end, but in actuality what I do next must be a beginning.

I remember the apostles who literally walked away from their jobs and families to follow Jesus. None of them knew what that beginning was about, or what it would lead to eventually.

My life today is an end of what I've worked for and a beginning of what will be. You are what will be. My immediate future is in Your hands as much as my eternal future is in Your hands. As always, I am completely, utterly dependent on Your grace and mercy.

So be it.

Now, what may I do for <u>You?</u> What would You have me do? I ask You in Jesus' name to reveal to me Your will for my life. What do You want me to know today, Father?

**Day 266**

Father God,

There's a new vein in the old gold mine! I feel like a miner who's gone back just one more time to make sure he got it all, only to discover a whole new vein!

I'm seeing myself apply an old talent a new way, and it's exciting to watch Holy Spirit amplify and exercise what You sent with my package. It's refreshing to know that the mine in my mind isn't completely mined out! Hope You don't mind the minded mine mind puns! Okay, I'll stop. I love a good pun and sometimes things are just too punny to stop mining easily.

I love the way You created us. You gave each of us an ability group of one or more kinds, and when we discover it, if we let Holy Spirit develop it, it can become amazing!

You set us up to be self-discovering! You are amazing! You have again astounded me! Wow! What do You want me to know today, Father?

**Day 267**

Father God,

How is it that I got myself into this mental dilemma? My mind is torn between the facts of what I know, what the word says, and my reality.

I find myself the target of other well-meaning people who want to help me. I feel a tiny bit like Job must have felt. People are telling me, "Do this." But they all have a different "this" in mind! But in all their telling, I have yet to experience the quickening that would tell me Your Holy Spirit agrees with any of them! Is there another option for me now? I want to obey. I want to be all You need me to be. But I am determined to do what You want, not just what would please men or women. It is Your praise I seek, not theirs. I want to hear "well done" when I come home, not "good job" from a friend. You are worth the best job I can do for You. So I ask, in Jesus' name, what "job" do You want me to do? What do You want me to know today, Father?

**Day 268**

Father God,

I remember being a child and being told "girls can't do that" many times. So I strove to do everything guys did. And I wasn't born with an acceptance bone, I think. It's not that I want to challenge things; I just don't want to accept what my spirit rankles at. It's made me a bad wife and poor mother in many ways. It's always been more important to me to do the things that really matter and not the "woman" stuff. I played with my kids instead of doing dishes. I chose kids over housework every time. But You know all this. I really am just writing to say thank You! I've been so blessed by enjoying every minute I've had with them, knowing I was doing what really mattered. Thank You for showing me that kids come before other women's opinions! And thanks for great kids who love You, too, now! What do You want me to know today, Father?

**Day 269**

Father God,

You amaze me. Everyday in some way You impress me with Your grace and mercy. You show me anew how much You love me. Every message I "stumble" across is a planned delivery from You. It has happened so many times that it is evident to me that You have orchestrated and coordinated a timely arrival.

You are the collator of our lives. As I travel and spend time together with You, I continue to learn of Your profound impact on me. The "falling together" of events is far too effective to be coincidental. People say that coincidence is Your way of remaining anonymous. I think You remain anonymous in order to continue to teach us.

I love the fact that You encourage me while not taking me out of the storm. I have to learn to manage while in the storm, not just how to escape from it. And no matter how bad it gets, I don't want to "bail" out because I know You won't give me more than I can bear. I may think I'm crushed, but life is just a feather on my head, compared with having to face an eternity without You. So please, in Jesus' name, bring on the lightening? What do You want me to know today, Father?

**Day 270**

Father God,

I'm still not surrendered! That doesn't surprise You, I know, but it does me—after all these years. For some reason I still want to do what *I* want to do. I still don't want to get in the yoke and pull Your wagon some days. Other days I get in the yoke and take off, going wherever my nose leads and dragging the wagon with me. You'd think that as many times as I've gotten the wagon stuck, I'd stop doing that. The driver sits higher than I can see and can see further. I need to trust You to drive, especially since my vision is getting narrower.

These days I don't see as many distractions as I used to, but I also don't see the arrows every time. I'm focused on the destination, but I also have to walk it. Help me to see the others on the road so I don't run over them?

Forgive me, Father, for all the times I've run over people in my hurry? My arrogance has hurt many, I'm sure. Help me to settle into the yoke and trust You to drive? I'll still get there, but I won't arrive with the skin of others on my feet—what a tragedy that would be! Help me do this right, Father? I ask in Jesus' name. What do You want me to know today, Father?

**Day 271**

Father God,

I'm so glad that You are not limited to where I am! You are so awesome! When I look at the circumstantial boundaries of my life, I see Your blessing. I didn't always see that. In fact, I've complained many times about my circumstances.

I would never have found You if I had not needed You. I'd settle into comfort and just roost there, much as I do in this wonderful recliner. I needed to be without things so I could desire and need the giver of all things. Thank You for not giving me prosperity!

To have You now more than makes up for all the "things" I did without. As hard as it seemed at the time, I know now that not one "thing" was essential to my life. I need Your presence, Your life, and Your power much more than physical things.

I love to seek the things which are above! Thank You for being where I can find You! What do You want me to know today, Father?

**Day 272**

Father God,

Still. Things are still here, just quiet, unchanging, immobile. And my life is unchanged.

My mind is churning, as usual, but my outward activity is small. What an irony I find myself living! The facts of my existence are beyond the comprehension of most people I know. The difference between what should be and what is has become a stress that is completely indescribable. It is so strange to have the tools I've always wanted, but be completely unable to use them! I feel like a man with no arms being given a plate of food that he must eat with a fork through a tiny hole in the wall. The good food is in sight but completely unattainable.

I have a unique request at this point, Father. Will You let me starve, please? And will You feed and care for the homeless, hurting, hungry and heartbroken in the world? Take what was planned for me and give it away? I'd rather give away than have so no one have it. I ask in Jesus' name. What do You want me to know today, Father?

**Day 273**

Father God,

Sometimes I wish for another voice, another vocabulary, or even another history. I want to worship You in creative new ways but I have only my life to draw ideas from.

You deserve all the ways we can think of to acknowledge Your great qualities. You deserve excellent expressions of songs, music, and verbalizations. Your gifts to us are so extensive and undeserved that we should spend our lives rejoicing!

Our minds are puny and our thoughts insignificant, compared to the vastness that is You. But in my minute, microscopically tiny way, I want so much to let You know how much I appreciate You. It is foolishness for the created thing to attempt to thank the creator, but I am a fool for You. I find that my heart's desire is to love, serve and bring delight to You in any way that I can. My mind tells me that I can't give You anything You didn't first give me. I can only do this. I give myself back and plead with You to accept all that I am, so that I may sit near You and rest on Your presence.

I ask in Jesus' name. What do You want me to know today, Father?

**Day 274**

Father God,

You have blessed me with so many simple treats! You have given us all so many things we love. I just traded treats with a neighbor—and our idea of a treat is so different! You have uniquely made us so each of us has our own preferences.

It is so fascinating that when we were given bodies, we all got a different set of taste buds. I'm still totally baffled by the folks who love raw onions! But I'm just as baffled by the sugar lovers. You truly gave us specialized equipment to help us enjoy the diversity of foods we would combine. And yet we have enough in common that we can nearly all enjoy garlic!

While I'm thanking You for taste, let me thank You for smell. I know smell protects us, but it also enhances our lives when it comes to good food. Thank You for our sense of smell.

Thank You for great food. I love the fact that even simple food tastes like a banquet to a hungry man! And I especially thank You for making cheap food tasty—and I do include beans! Until next time, thanks! What do You want me to know today, Father?

**Day 276**

Father God,

At the end of today, when its events have transpired, and I'm reflecting again on them, You will still be God. You will be awesome. You will be incredible and I will be amazed at Your greatness. Because I will still have You, I will be blessed. I will be loved and I will be able to worship You again. I'll be able to thank You again for helping me through a bad day or blessing me with a good day.

Until tonight then, I pledge to You that no matter what comes my way, I will not focus on the triumph, or the tragedy, or the mess, but I will remember You. You are awesome now. You are incredible and I am amazed at Your greatness. I am blessed to know You, I am loved and I do worship You! At noon You will be awesome, incredible, and I'll be amazed at Your greatness. This evening You will be awesome, incredible and amazing! Because no matter what I experience, my experience with You is that You never fail me, You never hurt me, You always provide for me and You always love me! Father, You are so God! Thank You!! What do You want me to know today, Father?

**Day 277**

Father God,

The events of my life have not shaped the building of my existence. My events are just building materials. Jesus is the foundation. My experiences, accomplishments and knowledge are the building materials that You will use to create a life work. Time is irrelevant to Your purpose. What I have done is irrelevant. What You will do is the relevant purpose. My only job is obedience. As I surrender to You my "set" of materials, I include knowledge, work experience, and life experience. You will use them and build them into the final production. I don't know what that will be yet, and at this point, I don't care. You are doing a bigger thing than I can see, so I trust You. Please, take my materials and use them for Your glory? Amaze those who love me with what You can do through me? I ask in Jesus' name. It was hard when You demolished my structure—the framework I had built for my life. But my toy production was nothing compared to the mega structure You will do.

Thanks for taking over. Someday I'll stand and shout—look what God did! What do You want me to know today, Father?

**Day 278**

Father God,

Many times I have heard, "We walk by faith and not by sight". My childhood church preached it as well as, "We don't walk by feelings".

I wish the speakers could know You as I know You now. Your presence is an addictive power and surge of love that consumes me within and without. I wish they could experience what I'm feeling now.

I know that others feel what I feel now. Now that I know that others are feeling what I feel, it makes me sick to know that so many are deceived into thinking that they shouldn't "feel" anything. I know that Satan's greatest lie is to convince people that You don't care; and You must be followed by blind faith. It is so obvious that he has cheated me and so many others out of this alive, vibrant, living interchange that You and I experience. In John 14:23, Jesus said he and his father (You) would come live with us. How accepting I was to believe that God Almighty (You) could live with me and I wouldn't <u>feel</u> Your presence! Please forgive me? And, Father, I ask You in Jesus' name to respond powerfully to anyone who asks You to let them feel You? What do You want me to know today, Father?

**Day 279**

Father God,

"...faith is the evidence of things not seen" (Hebrews 11:1b). This verse has changed many times for me. It used to be a "nonsense" verse—as in—this one is not making sense.

Then I came to understand it as "have faith and You'll see it" –which meant "hope You'll get it"—in my mind. But I've found a new truth. If I pray according to Your will, the request is a "done deal" as in—"it is absolutely, positively, going to happen"! I just must trust—and I do!

The only catch is to pray according to Your will. And now that part is much easier. Before I pray, I ask You what to pray! Why was I so dumb that it took me 30 years to figure out to ask "what" or "who" needed prayer? It builds me up to know that You will tell me how to pray by that wonderful, still, small voice of the Holy Spirit. And it is so much easier to trust You to just take care of every day. I only have to ask if I may pray for something. If You say yes, it's done! And if You say no, in Your wisdom, You see something I don't. And the best part is this, the evidence of thousands of answered prayers has built my faith to the point where I'll ask for anything You prompt me to ask, just to see You do it! You are so awesome! What do You want me to know today, Father?

**Day 280**

Father God,

Who knew? When I came to this town I had chosen it to be my "home town". By then I had already moved too many times. I didn't know I'd keep moving in this town. I think now of when I bought this house. It was my solution, but Your idea. Like so many things You've had me do—it has been perfect. My children grew up here and had only one address. I've spent my whole married life here. You know that even though I bought it when I was single, I'd be getting married, as You told me I would—a full four and a half years before it happened. I think You knew I'd need the security of a house, and that we would never be able to afford one on our own. You knew You would bless me with 18 years of poverty. You knew that this neighborhood would be perfect to rear children in. And You knew that a little house in a great town was just what I needed in this life.

You are so amazing! Because of this house, I've had a home for nearly 30 years now. I've had a security that has balanced the turmoil in my life. And I've had a place to run to in the storms. Now I have You and I release my little house to You and thank You for it. What do You want me to know today, Father?

**Day 281**

Father God,

Wherever I go, You're with me. Whatever I do, You're with me. They used to say that faith was stepping off a cliff, just knowing that You were there to catch us. I've stepped off a few cliffs in my time and I'm at a cliff again. Maybe it's my age, or just the fact that I'm settled, but this one seems higher than the others. The fall is farther and, if I'm wrong, the sudden stop really could kill me.

In the midst of this journey with You, one thing has been a constant. You have never let me fall—when I was obeying You. The problem is all the times that I thought I was obeying and instead went "splat". I'm still a little flat-faced. And that's okay, I've learned from it.

Which brings me to this question....

Will You, would You, please, make it absolutely clear to me that this is the right cliff for me to step off of? I have the faith to do it; I just need the confirmation that the step is obedience. I am so eager to continue with You, whether I continue as a ridge-runner or valley-vagrant, but, please, let me know whether to stay or jump? I ask in Jesus' name. What do You want me to know today, Father?

**Day 282**

Father God,

I'd like to thank You but don't really know how. I've discovered something that is probably a fruit of the Holy Spirit. Somehow, without my knowing how, I got a heart. It's new and I don't know where else it could have come from but You.

I've always known that I didn't care about others. My "self" was always the only important factor. But lately, without warning, I'm discovering that I care. Suddenly it matters if my neighbor with cancer had a good night. And I'm sitting here wondering why the cat so desperately wanted her favorite chair this morning, because it's obvious she needed a refuge. I wonder what scared her. And I didn't mind at all that she's in the chair I <u>need</u>. Do You see? Others, even the cat, are coming before <u>my</u> needs. That is so different!

I don't quite know what to do with the compassion stuff, and I certainly have no practice with it, but I'd like to thank You for it anyway. It seems to make others more comfortable around me, so that's good. I don't know when I got this heart transplant, but I like this one—so thanks! What do You want me to know today, Father?

**Day 283**

Father God,

You must be so weary of human justice—or injustice, I should say.

All humans know at least one story where the person in jail or prison shouldn't be there. I just saw on TV that one in ten incarcerated persons is there unjustly. I groan because I know that those same people, if they get out, will still be punished by our society all of their lives.

No wonder You said for us not to judge or we would be judged. And I see now why we are to visit prisoners. Not to mention that Christianity is the only guaranteed effective rehabilitation program. Now that I also have been unjustly condemned—not as a criminal—but as having violated a social norm, I grieve for others even more unfairly punished.

I know that this is an issue at the center of Your heart, because Jesus has been the penultimate example of injustice, having been whipped, scorned, spit upon, and crucified publicly, all without a crime.

Because of all this, I ask You to comfort the unjustly punished, love them, help them forgive their judges and betrayers, and release them into the joy of Your love? I ask all this in Jesus' name. What do You want me to know today, Father?

**Day 284**

Father God,

You amaze me. A door was shut and welded closed, but You are allowing it to open. It seems so strange to me. Truly, Your ways are beyond our comprehension. Nothing is impossible with You. Nothing is too difficult for You. When everything around me had collapsed, I was lifted up. You are too good!

Thank You for all that You do! Your wisdom exceeds our capability. I know that all things work for our future and are based on our eternity, and not our present. You know the plans for us, to give us a hope and a future. You bring us life now that is designed to prepare us for forever.

Thank You! We have no future but You! We have no hope without You! You are our dwelling place, our safe haven and our harbor. No one can stand alone or exist for themselves. You are the only one I love and my destiny. My life is defined by Your purpose and Your plan.

I need You! Everyday, every step, every decision I make is dependent on You. You are my source of health and my peace. You enable me, teach me, train me and lead me! You are—in all ways and at all times—holy, wonderful and perfect! What do You want me to know today, Father?

**Day 285**

Father God,

What's on Your mind? I cringe at that question. There is no human comprehension that could contain Your answer to that one. I think what I mean is, "What do You want to say to me today that I was so busy that I didn't listen for it?"

Have I missed a divine appointment? Did I fail You by not being ready to serve? I should not have been too busy to be available to You. I'm sorry. It seems I spend so much of my life apologizing for what I should have done. What can I do to better order my life and coordinate my activities? How can I direct my days so I accomplish more? A list is a good idea. Two lists are better. One for the things I need to do today and one for the things I can do everyday. I should put the housework on that one. But I must not forget more deliberate Bible study and scripture memory. Help me, Father? Give me structure and organization? I ask in Jesus' name for that and the answer to these questions. What do You want me to know today, Father?

**Day 286**

Father God,

So many days I waste whole days that I could accomplish much because I "follow my nose" all day. I forget to start my day by spending time with You and seeking You for Your will. It's three o'clock and I still haven't decided what to accomplish. Nothing gets done because nothing is attempted. It was easy when I worked full-time, because with little free time, I had to make it count. But with little work time, I let my free time float along and do little. It has truly been a break that I know I asked You to give me. When my life was chaos and insanity, You provided a wonderful respite. But my life needs direction now because I'm not using my time for Your glory. I'm sorry about that.

Help me, Father? Give me direction and purpose? Give me an occupation that provides income and puts me in contact with more people? I ask in Jesus' name. What do You want me to know today, Father?

**Day 287**

Father God,

With the plethora of makeover shows on TV, I'm thinking we should have some more....

Extreme Heart Makeover sounds good. Could we have a show where a person gets new heart parts and complete emotional healing? You would have to do that part, but it could happen, right?

Extreme Attitude Correction would be a hit with parents. They could call in a team of experts for one rebellious teen. I have some great ideas for that one, starting with cutting off all money.

How about Extreme Poverty Exposure? Take a group of well to do teens and have them live in families where they have to earn their money, do chores and be responsible for other family members while being denied common opportunities. It would teach them responsibility and compassion.

While these ideas sound good to me, I'm sure they won't happen. Life happens though, and many people will have real life experiences that will turn their hearts and heal them, fix their attitudes and teach them reality.

Thank You for life. It will never be a TV show, but we are learning from it. You are so awesome! What do You want me to know today, Father?

**Day 288**

Father God,

It's been days since I told You how much I appreciate You! I adore You! I'm concerned and worried that Your church doesn't see that they need to honor You above all. I write that and then realize that I fail You regularly. But I want the world to know that You are all-powerful, almighty, and totally able to blow us off the planet! So few understand Your greatness and Your love; You love us so much!

You hate to see us hurt but would rather see us hurt a little now to spare us from Hell later. Thank You for the occasional burn. Thank You for scorching all that is mine. I'd rather have a burn scar than burn forever.

Thank You for being the kind of parent that is willing to discipline. So many parents do not see that a lack of discipline is a disaster waiting to happen. Thank You for heading off the disasters in my life.

You are so awesome! It's good to know that after my "discipline event" that I can run to Your arms for love because You love me even when I've been bad. What do You want me to know today, Father?

**Day 289**

Father God,

You have given us so many truths!

I am astonished at the number of things You have taught me through the years. You have given us so many truths of scripture. It's as if each of us is a separate entity with a separate belief system and way of communing with You! It is evident that You do meet with us, but it is baffling why!

Every believer has his or her own beliefs that they insist are the one and only truth. In a world where infidels call us infidels, irony rules! Can it be that all of us are still loved by You? Absolutely! You are love and everything and everyone are Your creation. You are the only truth we can all count on (and the fact that You love us)!

I cannot accept so many of the convictions of others I know. But I can love the people. Help me to love them as You would love them? Put in me a desire to love all Your creation, especially the ones I perceive are "doctrinally challenged"? Help me to say to them what they need to hear to be able to hear You more clearly? And help me to hear You clearly so I won't be "doctrinally challenged"? I ask all these things in Jesus' name. What do You want me to know today, Father?

**Day 290**

Father God,

Okay. It's a new set. I'm in the pet years. I made it through my horrible teens, then the single decade, then the marriage revelation, then the baby years, then the park years. I survived the bike and sport years, sitting at ball parks and endless practices. I made it through learning to drive and others will hurt You, and now my kids come with four legs as the two-legged ones have left me.

The dog stole a snack from my purse this morning. It's no big event but it made news at our house this morning and we laughed as she hid under the bed. The cat can't spend enough time traveling and I'm a doorman for critters. Soon it will be the in-laws and then the grandkid years.

Am I learning all that I'm supposed to here? Have I missed lessons or opportunities? Should I be giving more somewhere or listening to someone else more? I'm sorry if I've blown it. Please show me the gaps and what I've missed. I should be old and wise someday—not just old. Help me to get all that I'll need? I ask all these things in Jesus' name. What do You want me to know today, Father?

**Day 291**

Father God,

My contribution to Your kingdom must appear miniscule to You. What tiny part I may play is of small consequence. But as I write this I'm reminded of the lepton—that tiny part of the atom that makes the atom possible. Without the atom, nothing is possible. Although I'll never see a lepton, or an atom, I know that to a scientist they are essential parts.

In some small way—perhaps as a grain of sand heated and destroyed to make glass, I can be a component of something big or lovely or useful. In some way, I know that we all have a purpose. We all have a place and a mission to fulfill. Just now I'm not sure what I'm doing here, but I am certain that You are certain what You have placed me to do.

So, for now, I'm going to keep putting along, learning about You, loving You, and trying to help people as much as I can. It's a little thing to do, but it's the best I can figure out, so please help me see if You have something bigger in mind? I ask in Jesus' name. What do You want me to know today, Father?

**Day 292**

Father God,

The last day of my life is coming soon. I know that it will be here when I least expect it and that it will not be known until it is over. I live with the knowledge that an end of my opportunity will come.

We all come with one shot to be a success at our given assignment. We are issued a number of days to complete it—although we can't be told the number or we would all wait until the end to work. And we have a dual assignment. The first part is to seek You and learn what we can until we discover the second part—and our work for You. I'm convinced that we must all do what we can to spread the news that You love all of us. Beyond that, each of us must fulfill a specific slot, doing what You knew only we could do.

In honor of the knowledge of opportunity and divine selection, I thank You for Your wisdom and Your guidance. You are so good to help us help You! What do You want me to know today, Father?

**Day 293**

Father God,

Today I will seek You.  Today I will seek You!  Today I will seek You.
Today I will seek You.  Today I will seek You.

I must follow, look for, seek after and desire truth to find You and I will.
Scripture says that if I seek You, I will find You.  I am on the trail and I'm
prepared to hunt until I drop, walk the soles off my feet, and whip myself into
action.  This is not an option to me any longer.  It is a life assignment.  There is
no "life or death" because death is only the beginning.  For now, I'm working
until the end, overcoming the obstacles, going over the barriers and ignoring the
distractions.

From the beginning You have offered me opportunity to find You.  From
the first day, You have dropped crumbs of truth and glimmers of light.  My job
is to do Your job.  No argument, no reasoning, no belief, no ideology, no
doctrine shall stand between us.  Relationship trumps religion, so no activity,
meeting, event or service shall create a diversion in my mission.  You are job
one.  You are my only focus.  You are my everything and I love You for it.
What do You want me to know today, Father?

**Day 294**

Father God,

You are my faithful, ever-present, awe-inspiring Father. You touch my life and bless my future. You correct my errors with love and engage me in eternal purposes. Your plan for my eternity is unrevealed, but it is certain. I look forward to it with joy!

Always listening, always understanding, You bless my present and enhance my prospects.

You are my one reliable source, my consistent companion, and my immediate responder. I thrill to the sound of Your voice and the knowledge of Your presence.

Magnificent organizer, You have choreographed my life into a dance of joy. You have removed me from the entangling vines and set my feet on higher ground. No obstacle obstructs my view or prevents my progress. You are my guide. You lead me in paths of righteousness. You remove from me loads that are not mine to bear.

I rejoice in Your all-inclusive plan that enables my success as a child of a king, You! Truly, You love me and desire to bless me. I love You. What do You want me to know today, Father?

**Day 295**

Father God,

I release to You my children. As we go our separate ways, I place them securely in Your hands, and fully entrust them to You, again, on paper here, now, hopefully, with Your help. Okay, so I'll never fully turn loose of my kids, but I'm cutting the strings and letting them decide when and how to contact me.

At the same time, I really need, desire, hope, beg and plead with You to watch, protect, keep safe, and oversee their lives.

I know this sounds a little amplified, but it is truly, undoubtedly, inarguably one of the toughest things a mother has to do, to turn lose of her children. I do not want to be an interfering, meddling, manipulative old lady who won't let her kids be adults. They have to be themselves, their way, so You can deal with them Your way. I know we have had this talk before and probably will again, but please help us all with this? Keep me from the phone and help them remember my number? Drop them hints to call their mother? I ask You to direct their lives and ask all this in Jesus' name. What do You want me to know today, Father?

**Day 296**

Father God,

Today I love You as much as any other day. It still gives me joy to know You love me. But today is hard.

I visited with a friend tonight who loves You so much. She is so looking forward to being with You. But tonight she is suffering. And tonight she made the decision, based on recognition of her physical status, that she is ready to die. She has cancer, and it hurts so much it keeps her awake at night. You will take her home very soon, I know. She knows that her family doesn't need her anymore. She knows that You will help all of them to make it through life. She wants to be with You so much. She has realized that her ties are cut here.

Please, Father, will You take her on home? Will You let her graduate? And all the other senior saints who are no longer needed and no longer find more than pain—will You please take them home also as soon as possible?

They have served You well and loved You well, please let their pain end? Let them enter in the fullness of Your presence? Let them come home? I ask in Jesus' name. What do You want me to know today, Father?

**Day 297**

Father God,

If I may, let me imagine that today is the first day of eternity with You.

As we meet, I see the love in Your eyes and experience the fullness of Your mercy as I recognize there is no judgment there. You will never cause me pain or sorrow there. The love we share is so welcoming and comfortable, I bask in its warmth and in the assurance that it is permanent. I realize Your heart is so big and so wonderful as it hits me that You love us all alike. I stand in awe of the majesty that surrounds me, knowing that if I walked forever it would not come to an end.

On this day, humans stand shoulder to shoulder with angels. We are bathed in waves of light as Your glory surrounds and encompasses us. I know that I never want to leave that love and would never do anything to hurt You. What joy it is to know that You have planned for this moment! What joy to know that You eagerly anticipated our arrival!

In this moment, I can only wonder what could possibly come next, but I'm absolutely certain that whatever it is, it will be delightful. Until that day, I will love You and love You and love You....What do You want me to know today, Father?

**Day 298**

Father God,

Now I see I was angry at You for years because I wanted to be teaching. I wanted to be the one up font. It never happened. In the back of my mind was the time I prayed, "Don't let me go until I'm ready". Now, I'm ready!

I got to go pray for jail inmates tonight and I was so up for it. And it only took 40 years to get me to that point! Considering what a mess I was when I started; it's a miracle I ever made it! You must have wanted to cancel me multitudes of times, especially when I thought I had arrived—like now—oh no!

But I know that this time, I'm doing okay, because I could tell that people were helped. That must mean I was submitted to You enough that You could work through me. Thank You for that.

It is so sweet to know that I've made progress finally. I'm reminded of the song—"No matter what the circumstances, what I feel or see, His word is working mightily in me." You have been working on me! I'm impressed with what came out tonight—You have done a lot of adjusting, correcting, teaching and training me! Thank You! What do You want me to know today, Father?

**Day 299**

Father God,

Thank You for Your Divine Delay—I was so touched tonight by the message You sent me via TV. The speaker spoke about divine delays—times when we are delayed for a season for a reason that may be outside ourselves.

And as I realized she was speaking to me for You, I loved her counsel. She told us tomorrow is in Your hands, but today is in our hands. And she told us to serve You now everyway we can. It's so true. I can't live hoping tomorrow will be better and just waiting for it. Today is mine to serve You and I will do it! In every way and every opportunity, I will serve You.

I'm so blessed to know that You have it all under control. You are so good! You didn't have to cue me in to turn on TV. You didn't have to let me know that my life is on hold for a reason. I would follow You anyway. I will love You anyway. But it is so good to know that out of Your supply of goodness, in the unlimited love of Your heart, You would let me know something that would build me up and help me hang on. Thank You, from the bottom of my heart. What do You want me to know today, Father?

**Day 300**

Father God,

Today I was so blessed by realizing that You let me be there for someone else—twice! Yesterday, I sat with a friend who had cataract surgery and was bored because she was unable to see well enough. We visited and had a great time. Today I got to go bake cream puffs with a lonely neighbor. She's been in a very hard place, so I've decided that when she calls and wants me, she gets me. My husband got mad because I didn't make supper, but he got over it.

And here's the surprise. We had a great time. Her children and grandchildren (and us) all got great cream puffs! She got to forget that she hurt; I got to bake, and since I don't have an oven it was great! And as I spend time with her, she lives a model of great Christianity to me! I'm the most blessed. I'm learning how to live a life that models You and in it I get to help others.

You have put me in a place where I'm available to bless, just so You can bless me! You are so awesome! Thank You. What do You want me to know today, Father?

**Day 301**

Father God,

Thank You for the good times! We had so much fun tonight! It was good to be with a group of fellow Christians who think like I do—that You are wonderful! It's good to meet with others who want to examine Your word and understand it like I do.

And it was so good to be able to laugh about it. We enjoyed the lively discussion. What a blessing to be with like minds and good hearts. You love us so much to let us share the joy with each other! You bless us too much almost.

I love the many memories I have of funny episodes at church and in groups like this one was. It is so uplifting to us to be able to laugh freely about our mistakes and "learning experiences".

Hopefully, You are laughing with us, or at least enjoying our enjoyment!

You have always been and always will be a great source of joy, thank You! You are my greatest treasure! You are my dearest love! You are my biggest delight!

Thank You so much for everything! What do You want me to know today, Father?

**Day 302**

Father God,

I have an issue I want to express to You since You know it already (You know the thoughts of my heart—right?). The issue is this. Sometimes I'm embarrassed when I can't pay. You know that I don't have my own source of income and am dependent on my husband. Since I'm not working, he feels justified in saying that I don't need money. I have to ask him for even my small needs. I can live with this, and with the embarrassments. But I would love it if You would let him know that my time is as valuable as his and that I should have equal rights to any free money we have, regardless of who gets a formal paycheck.

It occurs to me that many well-meaning and good spouses don't see money as a means of life and not as a possession. Like all things, it all belongs to You and we just get to use it.

So, on behalf of all abusers of power over money, will You forgive us and teach us better? And whenever possible, let each of us have our own source of income? I ask these things in Jesus' name. What do You want me to know today, Father?

**Day 303**

Father God,

Tonight my life is out of sync. Things are not as they should be. My family is acting out of order. My peace is missing.

Now, I make the decision. You are never out of sync or order. You are peace. So, I praise You in the midst of it. I thank You for the good that will come from it. I rejoice in the positives that will be produced because You have said You will sanctify us.

Thank You for all that You have done and are doing! Thank You for being love and giving me an anchor in the storm. Thank You for doing all that You do! You are awesome! You are whole and righteous. There is no division, no separation in You. Thank You for being all that we would ever hope for or desire. Thank You for giving me so much. You are so generous to give me the many gifts You have. You are so good to all of us.

I love You and I need You more than anything I've ever loved or needed. I need You more than I've ever needed You! You are so much more than more! What do You want me to know today, Father?

**Day 304**

Father God,

Thank You for surprise blessings! I love to find that something I have to purchase is half price. You are so good to us!

I love to hear from someone I was going to call but haven't had the time to do so. I love to go to church to discover we will sing the song I've been singing. And I'm delighted to receive something just when the need shows up! You are too cool! You supply my needs before I tell You! Thank You so much!

I love to do for others so much! It blesses me to know that You would use me to help someone. Yesterday that woman wanted to buy for me and I had to let her because I knew it would bless her to know she could bless someone! Thank You for teaching me to let someone else have the blessing of knowing they had blessed someone!

It is so good to know that You love all of us enough to let us experience loving one another. What a cold world it would be if we only loved You and You loved us.

I appreciate You so much—You are my joy every day in every way! What do You want me to know today, Father?

**Day 305**

Father God,

Thank You for all the things I never thank You for. I take so much for granted. Thank You for not ending the things we don't say thanks for. Thank You for clean air, much needed rain, pretty leaves, warm houses, good friends, great entertainment, and so much more!

You have always provided us with more than we need or deserve. You have always given to us, as ungrateful as we are. Everyday I have more to thank You for and yet it seems that I spend less time thanking. You are so patient with us. We have no patience with anything, but You allow us everything. We want "right now" action while You wait decades for us to do as we should sometimes.

Always full of grace, faithful and merciful, You are goodness. You express what You do every day in millions of ways. Thank You for being so awesome! Thank You for letting us know and be with You. I love You so much. What do You want me to know today, Father?

**Day 306**

Father God,

Do I fit somewhere else? I'm looking and I don't seem to fit anywhere here. My shape is out of shape with the shape holders I'm supposed to fit into. My form does not conform to any known form.

It can't be a design issue because You don't make mistakes, but I'm starting to wander about my placement. Am I out of place? Did I wander out of my space and into the wrong one? I never thought I'd feel orange in a black world. And I don't seem to be settled into anything. It's a strange feeling to realize I'm not compatible with "society" or my "peer group" or even my family. I seem to have been separated from all of the humans I know. I'm different from all of them. I know we are all unique, but I don't seem to even fit a category. How very perplexing it seems to me. But You know and I'm beginning to know that nothing happens without a reason. So today I trust You with today. And tomorrow will take care of itself. I love You and some day, if You are willing, will You explain to me what this phase of my life is all about, please? What do You want me to know today, Father?

**Day 307**

Father God,

Lately I'm noticing that our precepts are often flawed. It's so hard to explain to someone where I am spiritually because they've never seen the map! They listen but it is like I'm speaking a different language. Many people have a foundation that is missing some essential layers.

In spiritual things, I can't share what I know will help people because they don't have enough knowledge to receive it! It's like I'm trying to explain algebra to a first grader. Aaagh! I hate knowing that what I know would help them, but they can't receive it! You must be so frustrated with us sometimes as You try to get through to us!

You are all-knowing! You have all the answers, if we but knew the questions!

So, in light of my lack of light, will You please increase my understanding?" Will You please supernaturally input the knowledge I need to be helped? I'm willing to be helped. Will You please help us all to be willing? I ask in Jesus' name. What do You want me to know today, Father?

**Day 308**

Father God,

Thank You for the opportunity to be "provision" for my friend! Today I took a sandwich to a sick friend and she was so grateful she said, "I don't know what I'd do without You". Of course, I had to say, "You'd be just fine. I just happened to be God's provision method for You right now. God would have cared for You another way if it wasn't me".

I know that You care for us, Father, through many people and many ways. I'm so glad You are letting me help her a little bit. As a compulsive helper, it helps keep me out of other's lives! And it is good to know that my little bit is making someone else's life a little bit better.

But the neatest part is knowing that You are using me! It's so good to know that You trust me to be of service. Even on my good days the stuff I do is not worth much more than a dust bunny and to know that You blessed somebody through me really blesses me.

Thank You for the unexpected blessing of being able to bless. Thank You for allowing me to be one of Your helpers. What do You want me to know today, Father?

**Day 309**

Father God,

Our children are so independent, how have we made them so strong? They are so confident that they are ready to take on the world. How can we help them? I want so much to save them some of the pain of bad relationships and I accomplish nothing. They don't seem to hear wisdom. They don't absorb counsel these days.

Was I like that? Please forgive me if I refused Your input? Am I like that? Please help me to hear You clearly now; I want to grow and know You better. I'm so sorry that I've put up blocks to knowledge. I'm sure there were times that You wanted to teach me and tell me things and I just couldn't hear them. Please remove from me all obstacles to learning? Take away my self-sufficiency and confidence in my own knowledge? Show me what I need and how to pray it? Help me know how to learn? Open me up to receive all that You have to teach me?

I'm so stubborn and stupid in this—please help me get past myself to You? I ask all these things in Jesus' name. What do You want me to know today, Father?

**Day 310**

Father God,

It feels good to be at the end of a long project. I've worked long on this and it is good to look back and see a good work.

Do You feel satisfied at the work done on Earth? Are You finished with us? I'm happy to write that I'm sure You are not finished. Scripture says that You began a good work in us and that You will complete it, which tells us You are here for the long haul. You are continuously working on us while continually leading us. You are in control. You are the creator, executor/manager of our lives and the perfecter of our souls. You are wise, holy and in every way complete. You work in our lives to fulfill us as we fulfill our assignments. You teach us as we learn how to teach others. You help through us as we help with Your help! You are so awesome, so perfect, so fully and comprehensively above all that we need or could ask for that You overwhelm the mind! What joy it is to know that You know where we are, what we are, where we are going and what we will be. What a privilege it is to know You! Thank You for all that You are and always will be! What do You want me to know today, Father?

Made in the USA
Monee, IL
29 November 2024

71624990R00184